THE FELLOWSHIP OF BEING

THE FELLOWSHIP OF BEING

AN ESSAY ON THE CONCEPT OF PERSON
IN THE PHILOSOPHY OF

GABRIEL MARCEL

by

JOHN B. O'MALLEY

Notre Dame College of Education, Liverpool

THE HAGUE

MARTINUS NIJHOFF

1966

TO MARIE

FOREWORD

This book is the fruit of a critical inquiry into the nature and scope of Marcel's philosophic achievement. As such, it is concerned less with affixing the appropriate label (personalist or existentialist) to Marcel's thought – and with it making it stick – than with discovering the precise impulse and tenor of his philosophy. In the process of that more general inquiry, the writer found being forced upon him a central concept as integrating focus of Marcel's philosophic investigations. This concept was that of the person. Gradually it emerged as a concept not only of prime importance for understanding the underlying harmony that pervades Marcel's professedly unsystematic researches, but equally as one of profound significance for any philosophy that pretends adequately to account for human experience. Furthermore, it seemed that the concept derived much of that significance from its acceptance precisely in the context of Marcel's thought.

This feature of Marcel's philosophic writings alone is warrant enough for overcoming any initial embarrassment aroused in Anglo-Saxon breasts by his style. For, to speak candidly, that style is of a generation and a climate whose tastes little accord with palates trained to a greater astringency. Nor will Marcel's evident and unashamed concern with life and its problems necessarily evoke a warm response in minds accustomed to operate in an atmosphere of stricter and more academic reserve. The relevance of Marcel, however, lies not merely in the fact of his having first developed in France the themes of existence, situation, and the *corps sujet*. A sympathetic, though not necessarily for that a partisan, eye will discern in even such an early work as the second part of the *Metaphysical Journal* the anticipation of many questions that were later to exercise minds on the western side of the Channel. There we find him confronting the question of adapting language to its use in contexts deeper or transcending those of its normal usage, without completely severing its rooted links with the latter. There, too, he squarely faces the problem of the mind's relationship with the body, vigorously rejecting a simple dualism without falling into behaviourism or any facile suppression of one aspect of the situation. In the process, we find him demolishing the hypothesis of a ghostly doubling of physical action and can discern the virtual postulating of a defensible primacy of the concept of person. And, as a final instance, we find there the first steps traced of a path that was to lead to a satisfactory reconciliation and integration of the ontological with the moral point of view. All these questions were to be pursued by Marcel in a spirit freed from earlier idealist prejudice in a language continually readjusted to the situation it was called upon to explore. It were a hard arrogance indeed that found in all this enterprise nothing worth the further consideration.

It remains to thank M. Marcel himself for the characteristic courtesy and friendly interest he showed, both in conversation and in correspondence, in answering questions put to him concerning his philosophy. This book embodies work, later revised and somewhat amended, originally presented to the University of London and approved for the award of the degree of Doctor of Philosophy. My thanks are due to Professor A. J. Ayer, then of University College, who supervised the preparatory research and from whose clear and vigorous argument I greatly benefited. Any shortcomings in the work, however, I must sadly claim as only mine. Finally, I should like to thank my wife without whose encouragement the book would never have been completed.

The author has made his own translations from the French text, except where an official English translation already existed and was generally available. The following sources of quotations must, therefore, be acknowledged: *Metaphysical Journal* translated by Bernard Wall, (Barrie & Rockliff); *Being and Having* translated by Katherine Farrer, (Dacre Press); *The Mystery of Being*, I & II[1] and *Men Against Humanity* translated by G. S. Fraser (Harvill Press); and *The Philosophy of Existence* translated by Manya Harari, (Harvill Press). Where circumstances required a more literal translation by the author, this has been marked in a footnote.

---

[1] *The Mistery of Being* II was, of course, translated by René Hague.

BIBLIOGRAPHICAL NOTE

We have made use of the abbreviations listed below, when making reference to Marcel's works in footnotes to the text. Some of Marcel's works have been translated into English. In the event, however, we have found only few of these to be readily available. Of them *The Philosophy of Existence* has the advantage of presenting in one volume four important essays, two of which were separately published in the original French.

J.M.   *Journal Métaphysique.* (1914–1923). Gallimard, Paris, 1927. English Translation by Bernard Wall: Rockliff, London, 1952. The Appendix to the Journal, an essay on "Existence and Objectivity," was first published in 1925 in the *Revue de Métaphysique et de Morale.*

B.H.   *Being and Having.* Dacre Press, London, 1949. English translation by Katharine Farrer of *Être et Avoir.* Aubier, Paris, 1935.

P.E.   *The Philosophy of Existence.* Harvill Press, London, 1948. English translation by Manya Harari of: *Position et approches concrètes du mystère ontologique,* appendix to *Le Monde Cassé,* Desclée de Brouwer, Paris, 1933. Published separately by Nauwelaerts, Louvain, 1949. *Existentialism and Human Freedom,* 1946. *Testimony and Existentialism,* 1946; *Essay in Autobiography – Regard en Arrière* published in *Existentialisme Chrétien,* Plon, Paris, 1947.

R.I.   *Du Refus à l'Invocation.* Gallimard, Paris, 1940.

H.V.   *Homo Viator.* Aubier, Paris, 1945. English translation, under same title, by Emma Craufurd, Gollancz, London, 1951.

M.E. I.   *Le Mystère de l'Être I: Réflexion et Mystère.* Aubier, Paris, 1951. First Series of Gifford Lectures: Univ. of Aberdeen, 1949. English translation by G. S. Fraser, *The Mystery of Being, I. Reflection and Mystery.* Harvill Press, London, 1950.

M.E. II. *Le mystère de l'Être II: Foi et Réalité.* Aubier, Paris, 1951. Second series of Gifford Lectures: Univ. of Aberdeen, 1950. English translation by René Hague, *The Mystery of Being II. Faith and Reality,* Harvill Press, London, 1951.

H.C.H.   *Les Hommes contre l'Humain.* La Colombe, Paris, 1951. English translation by G. S. Fraser, *Men Against Humanity,* Harvill Press, London, 1952.

D.W.   *The Decline of Wisdom.* Harvill Press, London, 1954. English translation by Manya Harari of *Le déclin de la Sagesse,* Plon, Paris, 1954.

H.P.   *L'Homme Problématique.* Aubier, Paris, 1955.

P.I.   *Présence et Immortalité.* Flammarion, Paris, 1959. This contains: "Mon Propos Fondamental" (1937); "Journal Métaphysique" (1938–1943); "Présence et Immortalité" (1951); "L'Insondable," an unfinished play of March 1919.

U.A.   "L'Umanesimo Autentico e i suori presuppositi esistenziali." Published
            in the Review, *II Fuoco*. Jan.–Feb. 1958, N.1.
STUDIES   "What can One Expect of Philosophy?" English translation of address
XLVIII   given at Univ. College, Dublin – National Univ. of Ireland – on 11th
190   March 1959. The translation, by Rev. M. B. Crowe, appeared in *STUDIES*:
            an Irish Quarterly Review. The Talbot Press, Dublin. Vol. XLVIII No. 190.
            Summer 1959, pp. 151–162.
(For a full list of all M. Marcel's writings up to January 1st, 1953, c.f. *De l'Existence
à l'Être*, Roger Troisfontaines, S.J., Nauwelaerts, Louvain, Vrin, Paris, 1935, Tome
II, pp. 381, ff.)

TABLE OF CONTENTS

"Concepts lead us to make investigations,
are the expression of our interest, and
direct our interest."

L. Wittgenstein, Philosophical Investigations. I. 570.

INTRODUCTION

Any philosophy that pretends to some relevance to human experience, its description, interpretation, or evaluation, must at some time come to grips with the question of what man is and to what purpose, if any, he exists. Upon our understanding of the concept of person and of what it means to be human there depend not only matters of practical concern, such as the conduct of our lives and our behaviour towards other people, but also matters of theoretical concern, as is obviously the case with the human sciences. Positive anthropology – in the broader and older sense of the term – is influenced, wittingly or unwittingly, by philosophic anthropology or even, indeed, by its absence. As soon as we are faced with the problem of constructing a general theory of human nature or of human behaviour, the philosophic problem of man is involved.[1] Whatever we deem its function to be, philosophy is a peculiarly human activity; as such the concept of that function is encompassed by the concept of person. As inquirer, witness or, in one or other aspect, subject of inquiry, the person enters into the philosophic scene. Whether we conceive of the subject of philosophic inquiry as language or knowledge, action or being, the person is involved in his capacity of talker or thinker, agent or existent, our most immediate and familiar instance of any and each of these functions. What may be said of talking or thinking, of existing or acting, must be relevant to our own experience of these activities. Again, it is the person of whom we think as principle of every human activity, and the concept of person is consequently the theoretical focus of every inquiry of which such manifold activity, in its varied aspects, is subject. It is always possible, of course, so to define the scope and nature of philosophic inquiry that it becomes 'impersonal.' In making such a methodological decision, however, we either prescind from the personal as such or reduce it to an aspect or function of something else, denying it distinct

---

[1] c.f. Joseph Nuttin, *Psychoanalysis and Personality*. Trans. George Lamb. Sheed & Ward, 1954, pp. 248–9; I. M. Bochenski, *Contemporary European Philosophy*. Trans. Nicholl & Aschenbrenner. Univ. of California, 1961, (Paperback ed.), pp. vii–viii.

value and significance. In the first case, we should be in no position to assess the personal dimension of human experience, while our investigations would themselves fall subject to comment by an inquiry that did include the personal dimension within its scope. In the second case, our denial would have to be justified and, precisely, in terms of personal experience, while issuing in a fresh assessment of the latter and a revaluation of the concept of person itself, explaining in some new way those features of common experience that have been held to be irreducibly personal. A genuine understanding of the concept of person would seem, then, to be a matter of some philosophic moment.

The interest of a philosophy centred upon the meaning of the person will be more readily apparent when we reflect upon the rather summary treatment which this question has received in much of contemporary philosophy. Reaction to the Cartesian doctrine of the *Cogito* may perhaps have been partly responsible for this: taking this doctrine to be an attempt to establish a basic proposition, critical analysis has found it to be logically trivial.[1] Again, Idealism has tended to banish the Self to the regions of ineffable transcendence. In its turn, Empiricism, with its picture of the mind as a passive theatre of impressions, tends to divest the Self of substantial meaning. It were well to remark, however, that the concept of person is not co-terminous with that of mind.[2] Questions concerning body and mind, their reciprocal relationship and respective significance, fall indeed within the scope of an inquiry into the meaning of the concept of person, but this is by no means confined to their consideration. Again, confusion is often made between the question of individuality and that of personal distinctiveness: the person may be considered in his rôle of individual member of a class, whether this be humanity or some determinate social group; such individuality, however, does not necessarily coincide with his distinctiveness as person. Thus, the acceptance of the concept of person as that of a basic particular within our conceptual scheme does not exhaust its significance. The question remains of what we are to understand by this particular to which reference is constantly made in ordinary discourse. The significance of being the common focus of application for predicates ascribing material or corporeal characteristics and for predicates ascribing mental or spiritual characteristics has to be further explored and this in a dimension other than linguistic. At least, it cannot dog-

---

[1] C.f. C. B. Daly, "Metaphysics and the Limits of Language" in *Prospect for Metaphysics.* ed. Ian Ramsey. Allen & Unwin, 1961, pp. 180–185.
[2] C.f. P. F. Strawson, *Individuals.* Methuen, 1959, p. 133 et alibi.

matically be said at the outset that the situation of being such an entity is of merely linguistic significance.

Whatever one's theory be concerning the relationship of philosophy and language, it is clear that the adequacy of language used in dealing with the personal dimension of experience must be assessed in the light of that experience which it seeks to describe or to evoke. What we are really speaking of when we speak of the person; what is really there to be seen and what stance must be adopted in order to see it; how best to express what is then seen – these are mutually related and closely connected questions. They are all involved in the question of what it means to be a person. In raising this question, we obviously do not intend to deny that such words as personal names and personal pronouns are used with easy familiarity by ordinary people in ordinary discourse in the context of the routine transactions of daily life. Nor do we intend to deny that such people readily and commonly distinguish between persons and things. We raise the question in order to advert to the full significance of a familiar feature of common experience, because that very familiarity may blind us to the deeper implications of a situation in which, as human beings, we are involved. Whether we say that our concern is with seeing things as they really are, or with reality as such, or, again, with grammar in depth, is of little moment; what is of importance is to understand what kind of question it is with which we are concerned. The question itself may easily dissolve into several subsidiary questions, depending on whether our approach derive from a logical, an epistemological, an ontological, or an axiological interest. Thus, for example, we might envisage it as a question of how we were to secure uniqueness of reference in the case of persons, or how we could know that there were other persons and what they were thinking or feeling, or what were the essence of being a person or, finally, what constituted the unique value – if such there were – of the person. One danger in approaching the question in such piecemeal fashion lies in losing sight of the central subject of inquiry – the person as such – upon our understanding of which the correlation of the various answers to the more specialized questions must depend. It may be decided that such a piecemeal approach is the only feasible one, but such a decision could only be justified by considerations arising out of the more general inquiry. Furthermore, only such an inquiry could yield grounds for deciding whether or not the person presents a special case in the more specialized fields of the specific interests mentioned. There is, then, a particular interest attaching to a philosophy whose focus of inquiry is the person as such. It is the initial merit of Marcel's philosophic investigations that their concern turns out to be with the personal question as such and that they present this question in an original light that shows it to be a question of an especial kind. Their ultimate merit in indicating a suitable approach or in providing an adequate answer to the question remains to be seen.

The fact that the concept of person presents itself within the context of Marcel's philosophy as a concept of peculiar kind determines the method of inquiry into the meaning of the concept in that context. Such an inquiry comprehends a twofold task: that of understanding the philosophic context in which the concept occurs and that of understanding the concept as it occurs in that context. Such an understanding is obviously presupposed by any genuine attempt to assess the value of Marcel's contribution to the philosophy of the person in particular and to philosophy in general. In fact, the two aspects, just mentioned, of the inquiry are correlative. Context and concept illuminate each other. While the prior and detailed study of Marcel's philosophy as a whole has led to the conviction that its focal concept is that of the person, the present inquiry into the meaning of this concept in Marcel's philosophy offers, we believe, a vantage-point from which can be understood the orientation and structure of Marcel's philosophic inquiry as a whole. What we present, then, – to adapt the words with which Marcel prefaces his own brief study of Jasper's *"Philosophie"* – is not an exhaustive exposition of Marcel's philosophy but as careful an analysis as is possible, in terms faithful to its context, of a central idea that commands its development, mindful of Marcel's observation that what is of prime importance is "to assimilate *in itself*" its philosophic setting.[1] In return, there is the promise of a fresh and illuminating approach to the understanding of a concept that is focus of so many converging interests, both theoretical and practical.

Some preliminary comment can be made upon the character of such an enterprise. "Anyone who has not lived a philosophical problem," Marcel has said, "anyone who has not come to grips with it, cannot understand at all what this problem has meant for those who lived it before him."[2] To come to the question with a preconceived and rigidly determined notion of what is to count as philosophic inquiry or of what can be meant within its narrow terms of reference by the concept of person, intent upon the detection and denunciation of any heretical

[1] *R.I.* p. 284.
[2] *R.I.* p. 87.

deviation from one's cherished orthodoxy, may well confirm one's own prior conviction of its soundness and of the adequacy of whatever concept of the person it allows one to entertain. It will not help towards grasping what Marcel is actually saying nor, more importantly why he so says it, nor consequently, by viewing it in unaccustomed light, towards deepening one's understanding of the concept itself. The concept must be scrutinized within its Marcelian context in the light of common experience – though the meaning we can attach to this latter term must itself be critically appraised with reference to that context. Views divergent from Marcel's, of course, have their relevance, but precisely in their contrast to his own. So remarked, they necessarily display an anonymous character rather than the personal index that an equally scrupulous investigation of their originating context alone would permit them to bear. Ideas present in the reflections of other philosophers and which appear as themes of Marcel's reflection are of interest mainly and so insofar as they have been assimilated and appropriated by his thought. As such, those ideas that have acted a fertilizing principles of Marcel's philosophy, absorbed into the current of a reflection peculiarly his own, find a significance appropriate to their fresh philosophic setting. Thus, Marcel himself observes that while his essay, *Positions et Approches concrètes du Mystère Ontologique*, was written shortly after he had read Jasper's *Philosophie*, he cannot say how far that work favoured the development of its principal themes, while further remarking that not only his terminology but his whole spiritual orientation is different from Jaspers'. His opinion is confirmed by a reading of his own essay on Jaspers – especially of its conclusion – and by Ricoeur's comparative study of the two philosophers.[1]

There is another sense in which one might attempt an historical approach to the concept of person in the context of Marcel's philosophy, but which, on reflection, proves equally unpromising. That would be to attempt an account of the development of the significance of the concept in the development of his thought as a whole. In the first place, the "*Journal Métaphysique*" represents an emergence into that style of philosophizing which is characteristically Marcel's, without at the same time presenting those fundamental propositions from which a system might be developed. Apart from his stated aversion to the idea of systematizing the results of his philosophic investigations – the grounds

---

[1] *P.E.* Introd., p. viii; c.f. *R.I.* pp. 284, ff., esp. pp. 324–326; Paul Ricoeur, *G. Marcel et K. Jaspers*, Temps Présent, Paris, 1947, pp. 435–436; Lettre-préface by Marcel to *De l'Existence à l'Etre*. Roger Troisfontaines. Nauwelaerts-Vrin, Louvain-Paris, 1953. Tome I, p. 9.

for which should become apparent is the course of the present inquiry –
and his rejection of "formalism" in any guise, Marcel has repudiated
the view that his subsequent inquiries have been devoted merely to
the explicitation of ideas formulated in the Journal. What he is here
rejecting is the notion that his philosophy proceeds by way of systematic
and deductive elaboration from a set of clearly defined and basic
propositions. He does recognize that an underlying harmony unifies the
various themes of his reflection. That harmony is recognizable through
a thorough and sympathetic study of his philosophy as a whole.[1] In
recognizing its presence, a concept forces itself upon us as central to his
main concern and as focus of that harmony – the concept of person.
In the second place, however, this concept, as operative in Marcel's
philosophy, while it remains a constant and pervading theme of his
reflections, nowhere receives a full and explicit formal treatment that
integrates all the aspects it displays in the varying contexts in which his
reflections evoke it. Indeed, his essay on "Act and Person" could well
prove misleading as to the full significance of the latter concept in his
philosophy taken in its entirety, unless interpreted in the light of the
richer significance it develops within that wider context.

Our task, then, is to consider the concept of person in the light of
Marcel's present thinking, making use, if and when necessary, of the
development of that thought to bring out more clearly its present significance. In so doing, we shall be concerned with the more formally
philosophic of Marcel's writings. The project will involve in some degree
a rethinking of the various themes of which they treat and which are
relevant to a full understanding of Marcel's concept of the person, in
the light of this concept as operative in that context. If this means that
we must "examine, deepen, prolong" Marcel's investigations along
paths that he has opened up without fully exploring, this too has been
acknowledged by Marcel to be a necessary and legitimate procedure.[2]

We shall begin by indicating the central position of the concept of
person in philosophic inquiry as Marcel conceives this to be. This will
embrace an outline of the nature of such inquiry. It will also enable us
to understand in some measure what kind of concept it is with which
we are dealing. Subsequent investigation of the different levels of
personal experience will serve to bring out more fully the meaning of
the concept.

---

[1] C.f. Preface to Eng. Trans. *Metaphysical Journal*. Rockliff, 1952, p. vii; *H.V.* p. 7.
[2] *R.I.* p. 85 and in conversation with the author.

CHAPTER I

THE PERSONAL QUESTION

The philosopher's task is envisaged by Gabriel Marcel in terms of a personal research in which the ontological status of the person under-taking it is intimately involved. At the same time, the concept of person itself furnishes a focus of integration for a philosophy that is admittedly impatient of systematic presentation. These two features of Marcel's philosophy are in fact reciprocal. His whole philosophic development can be viewed, rather negatively, as a reaction to the abstract, ration-alistic, and impersonal idealism that was the keynote of his early thought.[1] More positively it represents a progress towards a concrete, realist, and personal mode of reflection. Instead of disengaging the person from the experience in which, *qua* experience, he is intimately involved, in order to reflect upon either subject or experience in abstract isolation, this mode of reflection seeks to "recollect" the integral experience by including the subject himself in the act of reflective with-drawal.[2] The precise nature of such a mode of reflection – "second reflection" as Marcel terms it – is not easy either to grasp or to explain. The effort to define clearly and simply what it means might well result in a distortion of the concept that misses its meaning. It would not be accurate, for instance, to describe it merely as an effort to synthesize the various conclusions reached by an analytic reflection. Yet, however, difficult the task of explanation, Marcel's concept of second reflection must receive patient and detailed attention in the course of the present inquiry. Not only has Marcel in mind this kind of reflection when he says that "philosophic method is reflective *par excellence,*"[3] but it is precisely this concept rather than that of "acquaintance with" – as contrasted with "knowledge about"[4] – which furnishes the key to an

---

[1] *P.E.* pp. 77ff.
[2] *P.E.* pp. 12–13.
[1] *P.I.* p. 20.
[2] C.f. H. D. Lewis, *Prospect for Metaphysics, (op. cit., supra),* p. 216, who rightly suspects that those who speak of an 'I-Thou' relationship, as we shall hear Marcel doing, in connection with awareness of other persons *qua* persons have something other than this distinction in mind. What Marcel does mean by this awareness shall appear in the course of the present inquiry. It is certainly not what Professor Lewis talks of as "a direct relation of mind with

understanding of what Marcel means by awareness of the person as such.

This concept of reflection is, in fact, correlative to Marcel's concept of the person as a being-in-situation. Furthermore, that situation, in his view, is a developing one: "'to be on the move' and 'to be in situation' constitute the indissociable modes, the two complementary aspects of our condition."[1] It is this "fundamental situation in which I find myself placed as a human being" which provides the point of departure for philosophic reflection as Marcel conceives it to be. Hence, he strenuously opposes any idea of a *Denken überhaupt*, because such an idea presupposes the notion of some kind of central vantage-point from which reality as a whole could be surveyed in its entirety, whereas it is in fact apprehended by each of us partially, in sidelong glances.[2] In the same way, he rejects the standpoint of Cartesian rationalism – though not denying that there are indications in Descartes' philosophy, if not in his successors', that might be developed in a non-Cartesian sense. In Marcel's view, the *Cogito*, as later Kant's thought-in-general, lacks any "anthropological index." Such thought is impersonal. It considers the human situation or condition as it might any other object, so suppressing it as condition.[3]

Is Marcel, then, advocating a purely subjective approach in philosophy? Such is not the case. This becomes clear once we advert to his criticism of "objectivity." The evaluation of personal experience as such, inherent in the idea of "an absolute point of view," operates in favour of an "objectivity" in contrast to which personal experience appears as "purely subjective." Now, within this context of subject-object contrast, "objectivity" develops a precise meaning that is quite distinct from its innocuous use as the equivalent of "what is the case" or "what is really so." It is this more precise meaning that the term bears within the context of Marcel's philosophy. That precise meaning, within this precise context, we shall have to define. Suffice it at present to remark that the pretension to objectivity implies for Marcel a certain attitude adopted, whether consciously or unconsciously, towards the subject of one's inquiry. Its keynote is 'insularity.'[4] The 'insularization'

mind" or as "a bare relation." The "knowledge about-acquaintance with" contrast belongs, in fact, to a quite different sphere than that which Marcel would recognise as the sphere of personal relationships. C.f. *J.M.* pp. 145–146.

[1] *M.E.* I., p. 149 (author's translation).
   P.I. p. 20.
[2] *P.I.* pp. 8–9.
[3] *P.I.* pp. 20–21.
[4] *J.M.* pp. 309ff., esp. p. 315–316.

of the subject of inquiry can have drastic consequences where the person is in question. It can issue either in an extreme objectivism or, and this correlatively, in an extreme subjectivism. If it issues in objectivism, experience is purged of its personal savour and, consequently, of the presence of anything that might irreducibly be termed 'person.' The latter dissolves into an agglomeration of states, perceptions, or qualities, to collocate which – or to relate them in some scarcely explicable fashion – becomes its feeble function.[1] If it issues in subjectivism, the self is either imprisoned fast in solipsistic solitude or divides into an absolute and concrete ego, between which it is difficult to forge any real and lasting links.[2] In any case, for subjectivism or objectivism, the person as such is effectively exorcized. In order to conserve any positive meaning of the concept, we must reconcile the persistence of the person with his fluidity, his distinctiveness with his fellowship; and this must be done without definitively crystallizing any of these aspects of the person, or of personal experience, in abstract isolation.

All this would suggest that the contrasting categories of subject and object are inadequate to an account of personal experience as such and that the question of the person's ontological status can only effectively arise beyond that dichotomy. That such is the orientation of Marcel's thought is evident from his remark concerning the suppression of the human condition as such by Cartesian Rationalism and Kantian Idealism: "A fictitious suppression; an abstraction that denies thought access to being."[3] The word 'being,' perhaps, sounds chill on contemporary ears. Possibly, it awakens fears of our being urged to take refuge in metaphysical abstraction or flight in mystical fancy. Although Marcel would readily accept the title of metaphysician, however, the term does not quite bear for him the associations it might for an English philosopher. For Marcel, a metaphysician is quite simply a philosopher whose main concern is with being. While the precise meaning of this term in the context of Marcel's philosophy remains to be fully explored, we may here provisionally claim for it a justifiable use to indicate a reality that, in Marcel's view, eludes 'objective' analysis and which must be approached with an attitude more amenable to its recognition than that informing such an analysis. It should be clear, at least, that nothing mystical or abstract is intended by 'being' from Marcel's

[1] For some of the difficulties facing this approach c.f. A. J. Ayer, *The Problem of Knowledge*. Pelican, 1956, pp. 198–199 and pp. 196–198 for a criticism of Hume's efforts to explain personal identity.
[2] *H.V.* pp. 190–191.
[3] *P.I.* p. 21.

insistence, already noted, upon our fundamental and concrete situation as the starting point for philosophic investigation. Again, there is insistence on our proceeding "by way of concrete approaches," making reference to "very humble, very immediate experiences," as well as his forthright declaration that the dynamic element in his philosophy is "an obstinate and untiring battle against the spirit of abstraction."[1] Finally, in his "Essay in Autobiography," he writes:

It was this concrete *ego* which I could not help regarding as the veritable *I*; for, when all is said and done, did not the problem consist in understanding its reality and its destiny? ...Was there not an arduous way which might give access to a higher empiricism and to the satisfaction of that need for the individual and the concrete which I felt in myself? In other words, would not experience be for me not so much a springboard as a promised land?[2]

This allusion to "a higher empiricism" and to experience as "a promised land," calls attention to two other, though related, features of Marcel's approach to the personal question. The first, implicit in the qualification 'higher,' is a rejection of traditional Empiricism. This is not surprising in view of his strictures upon the 'objective' attitude. We have already noted his rejection of the divorce between reflection and experience inherent in Idealism. It is on a par with his criticism of the Cartesian implication of what he terms "a severance... between intellect and life," whose result is "a depreciation of the one and an exaltation of the other, both arbitrary."[3] The rejection of Empiricism has a slightly different reason. Speaking of religious experience, but precisely as a personal experience, Marcel remarks: "We cannot be satisfied in saying with traditional empiricism that experience decides here as elsewhere; for the question is one of knowing *what* is this experience that must decide and how this experience must be, if one may say so, inwardly qualified."[4] Allowing for the difference in context, we might characterize the object of this criticism by what another philosopher, Merleau-Ponty, has named "le préjugé du monde."[5] In the latter case, the world in question is that of perception. The prejudice, however, that inhibits the recognition which Merleau-Ponty wishes to awaken, equally inhibits the recognition which Marcel seeks to stimulate. What is common to both philosophers lies in their insistence that there is a pre-

---

[1] *R.I.* p. 14; *P.I.* p. 23; c.f. *J.M.* Eng. trans. Preface. p. viii; *STUDIES XLVIII*, 190, p. 161.
[2] *P.E.* p. 78. This is the basis for Marcel's criticism of Fichte, c.f. *loc. cit.* and *H.V.* pp. 190–191.
[3] *B.H.* pp. 170–171.
[4] *H.V.* p. 13.
[5] C.f. M. Merleau-Ponty, *Phénoménologie de la Perception*. Gallimard, Paris, 1945. Introduction, Chapter III.

objective experience which empiricism, precisely because of its 'objective'
outlook, ignores. The importance of this recognition will become more
apparent when we come to treat of that essential feature of the personal
situation which Marcel calls 'embodiment' or 'incarnation.' 'Objective'
thought dissolves the *Meinheit* that pervades the experience of my body
as *mine*, substituting for the 'enfleshed' person a ghost in a machine or a
ghostless machine. The relevance, however, of the recognition of a
pre-objective experience extends to the personal situation as a whole.
It points to the presence of an *irreducible* within the person's experience
of himself as involved in that situation and as principle of his activity.
This allows play to a criticism of the contrasting notions of activity and
passivity and of their adequacy to a description of the person's role at
the heart of his situation and at the point of his insertion into the world.
The consequent notion of *receptivity*, neither purely active nor merely
passive, is vital to Marcel's reconciliation of what we have termed the
self's persistence with its fluidity. It also furthers the reconciliation of
the person's distinctiveness with his very real fellowship with other
persons, so providing an experiential basis for Marcel's equally important concept of *intersubjectivity*. Both receptivity and intersubjectivity
share with the concept of embodiment and that of *Meinheit* the character
of irreducibility. That is, their recognition derives from that of a personal
experience undistorted by the perspective of 'objective' analysis and
issues beyond the dichotomies operated by such an analysis. It is in this
sense that 'second reflection' is said, by Marcel, to be 'recuperative.'[1]
We have been introduced to one pole, to use a metaphor, by which
Marcel's reflection on the person is magnetised – irreducibility; its brief
consideration has just introduced us to the other – *transcendence*.[2] For,
if reflection starts with an experience 'below' the already organized
field in which objective analysis operates, its orientation is towards a
region lying 'beyond' that field. This is one sense in which the question
of the person may be said to meet with that of being; for being is "what
withstands – or what would withstand – an exhaustive analysis bearing
on the data of experience and aiming to reduce them step by step to
elements increasingly devoid of intrinsic or significant value."[3]

The theme of transcendence was already implicit in the notion of a
"higher empiricism." Marcel distinguished by its presence his own

[1] *STUDIES XLVIII*, 190, p. 162.
[2] C.f. *H.V.* p. 192. "I can say… that, from the beginning, my inquiry has been explicitly
directed towards the simultaneous reco nition of the individual and the transcendent, in
opposition to every impersonal or immanentist idealism."
[3] *P.E.* p. 5.

approach from the empirical: "pure empiricism excludes any idea of *direction*; under pain of giving the lie to its definition, it can only drift."[1] The idea of transcendence, in the sense of an orientation of reflection beyond the immediately experienced, is also implicit in the second phrase that drew our attention in the passage from Marcel's Essay in Autobiography quoted above: "experience would be... not so much a springboard as a promised land." Marcel explicitly denies that the philosopher should regress into a state of primitive naïvety.[2] While the evidence of pre-objective experience is neither to be misconstrued nor to be ignored, Marcel's "reflection of the second degree" is less concerned with immediate awareness than with "the first mediations by which this latter is constituted as experience."[3] Whether the 'mediations' be considered as effected by knowledge or by language is of little consequence. There is an uneasiness concerning an attitude that subtly determines what we shall see and how we talk about it: there is a dissatisfaction with the way things are said to be seen. The uneasiness, however, bites deeper than that. The philosopher is not just someone who is dissatisfied with the way in which others describe his position. He is like a man who has lost his bearings. The dissatisfaction lies deep within and with himself. "There is a sense in which it is true to say that the only metaphysical problem is: who am I?" And this, again, is not a retreat into solipsistic solitude. Even the problem of others is bound up with the problem of myself: "*if the others don't exist, no more do I: ...I cannot attribute an existence to myself that the others don't possess.*"[4] Even the more general questions that might trouble me, such as that of the meaning of reality itself, pre-suppose this question. "Who am I – I who ask questions about Being?"[5]

The question of what it means to be a human being seems to take on dramatic overtones. In a sense this is true. The idea of a "metaphysical disquiet" appears quite early in Marcel's philosophic development, to be precise, in his Metaphysical Journal. "A mind is metaphysical," he then wrote, "inasmuch as its position in relation to the real appears to be fundamentally unacceptable. Here we must take the word *position* almost in its physical sense. A false position." The disquiet is evidence of a "metaphysical need," to be sharply distinguish-

---

[1] *J.M.* Eng. trans. Preface, p. viii.
[2] C.f. *P.I.* p. 25.
[3] *P.I.* p. 20; c.f. *P.E.* p. 14.
[4] *P.I.* pp. 21–22; c.f. *op. cit.*, p. 114. For a similar reflection, c.f. Stuart Hampshire, *Thought and Action*. Chatto & Windus, 1960, p. 88.
[5] *P.E.* p. 6.

ed from mere "transcendental curiosity": "Metaphysical need is a kind of appetite – the appetite for being."[1] And later, in his most recently published work, "*Présence et Immortalité*," he asserts: "to be disquieted is to be unsure of one's centre; it is to seek one's centre, ones balance... these words sufficiently mark the fact that philosophy, such as I conceive it to be, is a development that is pursued within the subject, considered as a spiritual organism, but yet within the reality of which this subject is the aim – I would even be tempted to say the stake, so much does this development seem to me like a gamble or a drama."[2]

Some qualification concerning the nature of Marcel's philosophical approach to the question of the person is imperative in view of his assertion of its transcendental orientation. It would, for instance, be premature summarily to dismiss his approach as purely eristic, merely because the person and his destiny appear to him in a dramatic light. Substance might seem to be lent to the charge by the fact that Marcel is also a dramatist, whose dramatic work has had some bearing on his philosophy. This influence, however, should not be exaggerated. He himself has asserted that his plays do not derive from his philosophy. Neither can his philosophy be said to derive from his plays. While he admits that certain ideas, which find a more formal development within his philosophic investigations, first presented themselves dramatically to his attention, Marcel professes a profound mistrust towards philosophic drama. "A philosophy, once elaborated, has nothing to gain from being dramatically expressed and... it can scarely be so expressed without distortion."[3] Similarly, he draws a clear line of distinction between philosophy, and this includes a philosophy like his which is open to the transcendental implications of the human condition, and religion. There may be, and Marcel would say that there is, a secret convergence between the two. The instrument of research, however, in each case is different. "Religion, in effect, can only be based upon Faith. The method of philosophy, I think, is, on the contrary, reflection." The Faith in question is, of course, theological Faith, the ground for whose acceptance is Divine Revelation. Belief does play a part, an important part, in relation to Marcel's understanding of the concept of person. To consider the matter in detail here, however, would be to complicate unnecessarily this preliminary survey of his approach to the personal question. All we need do at present is to stress

[1] *J.M.* p. 279.
[2] *P.I.* pp. 21, 23.
[3] Broadcast Introduction to Radio Performance of "La Chapelle Ardente". Radio Éireann, Dublin, 1959, (Trans. by author).

the sharp distinction in Marcel's philosophy between such a belief and theological Faith. Reflection on the person is not based upon Revelation, nor is it intended by Marcel as an introduction to, much less as a substitute for, religion.[1]

Why, then, speak of a convergence between philosophy and religion? Now, it is a matter of fact, and one that had better be stated and its relevance discussed in order to avoid misunderstanding, that Marcel is a convinced Christian. Furthermore, his philosophic reflections have played their part in opening his mind to the acceptance of Christianity, at least in the sense that they proved no obstacle to that acceptance. It is natural, too, that with a philosopher like Marcel, who believes that one cannot step out of one's concrete situation in order to philosophize impersonally, his faith should quicken his mind to certain features of that situation which, otherwise, he might ignore. On the other hand, that concrete approach itself, in conjunction with his expressed desire to safeguard the independence of philosophy, make him more aware of the possibilities of dogmatic prejudice and less likely to succumb to them. In fact, there is no appeal to dogma anywhere in Marcel's philosophy: his philosophy must be assessed on purely philosophical grounds, as he himself would agree. Nonetheless Marcel quite reasonably asserts that just as we cannot in our reasoning ignore the centuries of positive science, neither can we afford to ignore those of Christian thought. "But neither the existence of Christianity nor that of positive science plays in this connection more than the rôle of a fertilizing principle."[2] It is quite simply a matter of historic fact that Christian thought, either in its acceptance or in its rejection, has influenced Western philosophy. It is not surprising, therefore, that in so central a question as that of the meaning of the concept of person, there should arise points for consideration that also concern thinkers in the Christian tradition, working in a purely religious context. All that can be reasonably asked is that such points of mutual interest be treated by Christian philosophers in purely philosophic terms. Nor can there be any objection to a philosopher's belief that his purely philosophic investigations issue in harmony with his religious faith. The reality of that harmony is a matter for theological, not philosophical, judgment. Provided the philosopher's investigations are truly philosophic, any affinity existing between his findings and dogma is, in the philosophic context, merely

[1] *STUDIES XLVIII*, 190, pp. 161–162.
[2] *P.E.* pp. 30–31; c.f. F. C. Copelston, *Contemporary Philosophy*. Burnes Oates, 1956, pp. 172–173.

incidental: philosophically, it is an argument neither for nor against his conclusions. Finally, we may remark that while Marcel makes use of terms – such as incarnation or mystery – that have a theological use, for him they have a purely philosophic significance within the context of his philosophic investigations, quite distinct from their meaning in a theological context.

The idea of transcendence enters into the philosophical discussion of the concept of person with the recognition that the fundamental situation in which we find ourselves is a developing one and that, correlatively, reflection upon that situation must progress beyond the data of immediate awareness. Having said so much, we must now try to give a rough indication of what transcendence may mean when the term is applied to the person. There is no question, for Marcel, of going outside or beyond experience. If the word 'transcendence' is to have any meaning, he asserts, there must indeed be a possibility of experiencing the transcendent as such. At the same time, the possibility of such an experience is greatly increased for him by the recognition that experience is not limited to what is furnished by the external senses.[1] So much we might have expected from Marcel's rejection of traditional empiricism. It is, of course, a claim that shall have to come under further scrutiny. The concept of the subject's 'receptivity' – as opposed to a mere passivity or to a pure activity – is, however, a sufficient indication of a fresh and promising approach to the question. On the other hand, this concept also gives indication that reflection on the person is not to be thought of in terms of an eidetic intuition. For one thing, Marcel heartily distrusts the term 'intuition.'[2] The very term reflection, so constantly in use by Marcel, implies for him an effort and progress that accords ill with intuition: "I note... that my method seems to consist in the alternation of a sort of prospection with a reflection that analyses and criticizes what has been given thanks to the initial prospection."[3] Then, again, there can be no question of an existential *epoche* or 'bracketing' of existence. For Marcel, existential and personalist interests are closely linked. 'Existence' itself is used by him to denote the fundamental situation in which the person finds himself prior to any analytic reflection. As such, it is irreducible in character and its features are discoverable only to a reflection free of 'objective' prejudice. Certain of those features have an immediate

---

[1] *M.E.* I, pp. 55–56.
[2] *STUDIES XLVIII*, 190, p. 162.
[3] *P.I.* p. 48, n. 1.

bearing on the point at issue. For Marcel, existing, awareness of the self as existing, and awareness of the self as incarnate cannot really be separated.[1] This means that the person as existent is isolated neither from the world in which he is situated nor from other persons who inhabit it. This does not entail a denial that problems concerning the existence of things or of persons can arise; but it does indicate how, in Marcel's view, such problems do arise. Broadly speaking, they arise because 'objective' analysis 'dissolves' the integral character of the existential situation. It then becomes increasingly difficult to 'recover' the lost unity of the self, the close bond uniting the embodied self with the world, and the 'intersubjective' communion of presence that binds him to his fellows. The 'recuperative' effort of second reflection is not, however, a synthetic activity, pure and simple. It is impossible, for instance, to forge an 'intersubjectivity' out of a collection of objects, considered precisely as such. The movement towards transcendence, therefore, involves a change of attitude on the philosopher's part. He must switch from an objective attitude, adapted to the consideration and solution of 'problems,' to an attitude more suited to the entertaining and answering of questions that are 'metaproblematic' in nature. While a 'problem' may be confronted with detachment and even require, for its adequate solution, a strict disinterest on the inquirer's part, a 'metaproblematic' question involves him in such intimate fashion that his own ontological status comes into question. That is, such a question includes within its scope the person as a whole; its answer bears upon his essential meaning, his nature and his destiny.[2]

The concept of person, so envisaged, emerges as the answer to a 'total' question issuing in something like an 'ultimate' meaning. It is as a search for an answer to a total question that Marcel qualifies his investigations as 'metaphysical.' "To raise the ontological problem is to raise the question of being as a whole and of oneself seen as a totality."[3] We have already remarked that, for Marcel, any attempt to raise the question of 'being as a whole' involves the question of 'who am I who question being?'. Here, then, is an inversion of the usual 'metaphysical' process. Instead of tackling the question of 'being as such' and then fitting the person into the resulting scheme, Marcel sees the personal question as primary. This, again, is the sense of his qualifying the question as a 'mystery.' "A mystery is a problem which encroaches

[1] *B.H.* pp. 10–12.
[2] *B.H.* p. 171, *M.E.* I, pp. 227–228.
[3] *P.E.* p. 7.

upon its own data, invading them, as it were, and thereby transcending itself as a simple problem."[1] The terms 'metaphysical' and 'mysterious' really coincide with 'metaproblematic.' It would, perhaps, be preferable to use the latter term to avoid confusion with extra-philosophical uses of the other terms and to allay suspicion that we are being led into the mystical regions of 'what cannot be talked about.' However, just as Marcel insists that there must be an experience of the transcendent, if this word is to have a meaning, so also would he admit that, if there be an experience, we must be allowed and prepared to talk about it. "What I wanted to know," Marcel states in an autobiographical passage, "was not so much what reality is, as what we mean when we assert it."[2] Such a statement might well seem to accord with an analytic approach, conceptual or linguistic. Marcel is indeed concerned with what we mean when we speak of personal experience – with what we say about the experience of being a person. This meaning, nonetheless, ultimately must be assessed in the light of that experience itself. The whole question, then, turns upon what this experience is taken to be. Now, reflection is the process in which we question experience; so that the questions we raise and, consequently, the answers we get depend in great measure upon the attitude we adopt, wittingly or unwittingly, towards its subject in the very process of reflecting. At the lowest level of interpretation, the concept of person has as its basis a situation whose fundamental feature is personal involvement: "being 'involved' is the fundamental fact; I cannot leave it out of account except by an unjustifiable fiction, for in doing so, I proceed as though I were God, and a God who is a mere onlooker at that."[3] A reflection that seeks to understand the concept of person must take into account this factor of personal involvment. This is the meaning of raising the question of "oneself seen as a totality." It betokens a refusal to ignore the 'appropriation' that makes experience personal or to reduce that experience to any one of its aspects and, at the same time, it betokens a readiness to explore fully the implications of such an appropriation. The objective attitude is unable to accommodate without distortion the integral nature of personal experience, if indeed it does not ignore altogether this fundamental feature of the person. It is Marcel's contention that the only alternative to adopting that attitude is to adopt the metaproblematic.

We have remarked that 'second reflection' – that mode of reflecting

[1] *P.E.* p. 8.
[2] *P.E.* p. 80.
[3] *P.E.* p. 9.

informed by the metaproblematic attitude – cannot be represented simply as a synthetic activity. It might, for instance be argued that the integral quality of personal experience could be preserved by a reflection that sought to re-integrate the various conclusions about the person at which scientific inquiry and objective analysis would arrive. Marcel would reject such an argument on two counts: the nature of scientific inquiry itself and the nature of an objective system as such. The whole trend of scientific inquiry is towards specialization. Although attempts at synthesis will always be made, these syntheses must appear relatively adventitious with respect to the specialized sciences themselves. Moreover, since the sciences are distinct and multiple, they are less effective as sciences the more they are brought to bear on a question where division into watertight compartments no longer holds. If, however, we raise the question of the person, even if we raise it as of the subject who conducts these various specialized inquiries, he will be viewed as the object of possible sciences. Furthermore, as object of applied science, the subject can only enjoy "a reflected light, a light borrowed from objects, since the sciences to be applied to him will inevitably be constructed on the model of sciences directed upon the external world."[1] There is no question here of condemning science as such. What is condemned is the adoption of the scientific attitude in face of a question that lies outside the competence of scientific inquiry. In its own field, scientific inquiry, properly conducted, can lead to valid conclusions and the scientific attitude is in order. It is only when an omnicompetence is claimed for scientific method, especially when this claim is extended to the adequate accounting of personal experience as such, that the scientific attitude must be rejected as inept and unsatisfactory. There is, likewise, no suggestion that the metaproblematic mode of reflection is appropriate to the purposes served by scientific research. This qualification extends to the remarks made about specialization. "Doubtless it is legitimate," Marcels says, "to establish certain distinctions within the unity of the being who thinks and endeavours to *think himself*; but it is only beyond such distinctions that the ontological problem can arise and it must relate to that being seen in his all-comprehensive unity."[2]

Marcel's antipathy to the very idea of an objective system of thought is strongly marked. This antipathy derives from his own philosophic experience. At one time he did envisage the composition of a "dogmatic

[1] *B.H.* pp. 187–188.
[2] *P.E.* p. 7; c.f. *H.C.H.* pp. 46–47.

work" in which he hoped to set down in close logical connection the essential theses to which his own investigations would have led him to subscribe. Thirty years after writing the "Metaphysical Journal," which was intended as the preparation for such a work, Marcel admits, somewhat ruefully, that the project would never be realised. The preparatory work had come to stand by itself, like his subsequent investigations, as "an instrument of research that is an integral part of the inquiry itself."[1] What Marcel means by this is that a philosophical inquiry, of the kind in which he is engaged, does not issue in the discovery of "particular truths" which can be isolated from the continuing process of inquiry, in order to form the basis of a series of abstract deductions. The philosopher, according to Marcel, is continually calling into question whatever conclusions he arrives at and constantly referring them to the concrete situation that is the subject of his inquiry. It is clear that philosophic inquiry, so conceived, is identical with what Marcel terms a metaproblematic investigation. "It is characteristic of a particular truth," he writes, "to be capable of strict formulation and it runs the risk of being confused with the statement in which it is resumed or, more precisely, of offering no resistance to such confusion which is, perhaps, a corruption. In so far at it is taken in itself, that is independently of the inquiry from which it issues, it tends to appear as external to the subject... The rôle of philosophic reflection will be to make apparent the fallacious character of any particular truth, if it be reduced to an element that can be isolated from its knowing."[2]

One might be tempted to see in Marcel's concern for "the integrity of the real" and his insistence upon the recuperative function of reflection the influence of an Idealist Monism. Marcel, it is true, admits to a sympathy with Bradley's criticism of theories of relations current in his time. At the heart of such sympathy, however, there lies a belief that any theory of relations which envisages them as some kind of makeshift bond between monadic substances does scant justice to the wealth of experience underlying personal relationships as we actually live them. If he prefers to speak of 'super-relations,' it is in order to stress the 'non-objective' character of the relationship existing between a person and his body or between one person and another. The full meaning of a relationship so conceived will have to emerge from consideration of its various instances in the course of our present inquiry; but, just as Marcel envisages a receptivity that transcends the opposition of activity

[1] *R.I.* p. 86 *J.M.* Eng. trans. Preface, p. xii; *H.V.* p. 5.
[2] *P.I.* p. 16.

and passivity, so does he envisage a relationship that transcends the
opposition of internal and external, where this contrast no longer
holds, since it belongs to the sphere of problematic reflection. He is,
at the same time, equally critical of any attempt to dissolve appearances
in an Absolute Reality. If he is convinced, partly as a consequence of
his perusal of Bradley's writings, that "reality cannot be summed up,"
he is prepared to concede a negative value to outright Pluralism as a
necessary protest against any illicit idea of integration. Indeed, Marcel
finds little of ontological significance in the classic contrast of the one
and many. In its place, he would invoke the contrast of the 'full' and
the 'empty.' This contrast, besides, serves to indicate the sharp and
radical distinction between the "person seen as a whole" and the abstract totality of the Monists. More significantly, it shows that, with
Marcel, the stress is away from personal distinctiveness conceived in
terms of numerical identity – an identity to be preserved or to be
dissolved at all costs – to personal distinctiveness conceived in terms of
fulfilment and value.[1]

The notion of value is of especial significance in elucidating the
orientation of Marcel's inquiry into the meaning of the concept of
person. At the present, however, we must content ourselves with some
further observations concerning his mistrust of objective systems of
thought, which are not without relevance to the question of value itself.
Value, as Marcel justly observes is a polymorphous concept: "it can
be presented as truth or justice, and it concerns different aspects for
the artist as for the believer." It is relevant both in a speculative and
in a practical context and has various fields of application within those
contexts. Fundamentally, however, the concept of value corresponds
to that of fulfilment or plenitude in Marcel's philosophy – it is "in
contrast with exhaustion in all its forms."[2] It is at once clear that value
so understood cannot be satisfactorily accommodated within an
objective system, abstract and impersonal. Once again be it understood,
Marcel raises no objection to abstraction as a purely methodological
device of strictly defined purpose and limited scope. We must, nonetheless, in his opinion, retain a precise and distinct awareness of the
methodological omissions deemed necessary for obtaining an envisaged
result. The danger always remains of yielding to "a sort of fascination,"
under whose influence we cease to be aware of the pre-abstractive
situation, within which abstraction itself operates, to consecrate as an

[1] *J.M.* Eng. trans. Preface, pp. xi–xiii; *P.E.* pp. 14–15; *H.C.H.* p. 94; *M.E.* I, pp. 15, 16.
[2] *J.M.* Eng. trans. Preface, p. xi.

absolute principle of inquiry what was merely a method, if not simply an expedient. When that happens, we are no longer dealing with a simple process or technique; we are confronted with the operation of what Marcel terms "the spirit of abstraction" – that is, of an emotive attitude that prejudices reflection. This spirit of abstraction, according to Marcel, breeds a kind of contempt for the concrete conditions of personal experience. This is especially true of the derivative process of reduction, whereby recognition is withheld from anything of irreducible or distinctive value in the person as such. Speaking of general formulae of the type "This is only that..." or "This is nothing else than...", Marcel remarks: "Every depreciatory reduction of this kind has its origin in resentment, that is to say, in passion, and basically corresponds to a violent attack upon the integrity of the real – an integrity to which only a resolutely concrete mode of thinking can do justice."[1]

This charge against the integrity of the real echoes Marcel's claim that by leaving the fundamental fact of my involvement in experience out of account "I proceed as though I were God." Yet the use of such phrases issues from a purpose more serious than an attempt to heighten through rhetoric the temperature of philosophic argument. At the root of Marcel's indictment of attempts either to construct an objective system or to unduly extend the scope of scientific technique is a recognition that interpretation of experience is never a neutral seizure of a datum. As we have earlier remarked, philosophy, whatever our understanding of its function, is an activity: as such, it involves the taking up of a position with regard to the world, and, consequently, to ourselves and other persons who inhabit it. The mere fact of including or excluding certain topics from the field of meaningful discourse involves a decision, whether explicit or no, concerning their relevance not only for the type of discourse initiated, but also for the person initiating it. There is, indeed, a sense in which it is true to say that philosophy leaves things as they are, but only if we intend and succeed by our inquiry in seeing them as they are. In order to so succeed, we must be ready to declare our prejudices, not least to ourselves. Marcel is concerned with the prejudice informing alike attempts to "incapsulate the universe" within a rational and objective system or to subject the person to techniques, scientific or linguistic, that are radically impersonal. As previously remarked the objection is not to scientific investigation as such, provided it be conducted within its own strictly limited field, nor to its investigation of those aspects of human experience or human

[1] *H.C.H.* pp. 115–116.

reality that lie within its limited scope, provided again that this scope be not extended to include the person, precisely *qua* person. The trouble is, however, that such a restriction is difficult to observe in practice, not least because the desire to unify is strong, if not the main impulse to intellectual inquiry. The process of rationalization must be rationally controlled. Thus, it is in the name of intelligence that Marcel opposes "the spirit of abstraction" which – as an attitude of mind, to be sharply distinguished from the simple method of abstraction – represents an impulse to rationalize run wild: "The spirit of abstraction is essentially of the order of the passions; it is passion, not intelligence, that forges the most dangerous abstractions."[1] It might, of course, be objected that by prescinding from what Marcel would term the "personal index" of experience, no theory is advanced or implied concerning the person. If such were indeed the case, Marcel could scarcely object, provided, that is, no attempt were being made to argue from so restricted a viewpoint to the meaning of the concept of person or without making the readjustment of attitude necessary for taking into account the person's fundamental involvement in his experience. It frequently happens, nonetheless, that the restriction of scope inherent in the very nature of an impersonal inquiry – which Marcel would deem quite proper to an investigation of the problematic – is canonized as an essential characteristic of philosophic inquiry as such. A criterion of meaningfulness is then elaborated that rules out in advance the kind of answer that metaproblematic inquiry alone can furnish. In such case, of course, the outcome of the investigation is prejudiced. Now, while it always remains possible to plead a simple agnosticism with regard to the person as metaproblematically conceived, such ignorance, although an estoppel to further inquiry along that line, is only such for the pleader and provides no warrant for barring others from proceeding with it.

It would appear, then, that inquiry into the meaning of the concept of person is for Marcel a special kind of inquiry. Furthermore, that kind of inquiry, which, using a term of Marcel's, we have named metaproblematic, involves a peculiar assessment of the kind of question posed by its subject and the adoption of a distinctive attitude towards personal experience. Our next task must be to examine more closely what is meant by metaproblematic inquiry and how it is distinguished

---

[1] *H.C.H.* p. 9; one must be careful here to distinguish "passion" from "emotion" – the passion here in question is what Professor J. MacMurray would describe as, "Irrational emotion": c.f. his *Reason and Emotion*. Faber, 1935.

from that problematic inquiry with which it is contrasted. This we shall do with reference to that fundamental situation which Marcel sees as the basis of the concept of the person – the situation of a human being, embodied, in the world. Our immediate concern will, however, be with the manner in which such a situation must be approached rather than with its detailed analysis; and here we will be concerned with the meaning of the distinction that Marcel draws between 'being' and 'having.' Once we have gained insight into the general nature of metaproblematic inquiry, the kind of reflection it involves and the distinctive features of the kind of concept it works with, we can usefully proceed to the analysis of the personal situation in depth.

CHAPTER II

METAPROBLEMATIC INQUIRY

The several strands in Marcel's argument directed against the adoption of an objective attitude in the assessment of personal experience as such and against the undue extension of scientific method to the solution of the personal question would seem to marry in the assertion that something like a category mistake is operative in such ways of envisaging the concept of person. The categories confused are those of 'being' and 'having.' The term 'category,' of course, is patient of varied interpretation. In the present instance, there is certainly implied a difference in kind or use between concepts of the one and the other category: the concept of body, for instance, – which is of no little importance in the elucidation of the concept of person, as both common experience and common usage (witness such expressions as 'somebody' or 'anybody') should lead us to suspect – has a distinct use and a different shade of meaning in the context of "the body I have" to those it enjoys in the context of "the body I am." Yet, as this same instance testifies, the difference in usage or meaning derives from a difference in the attitude with which the situation evoking the concept is approached.

In the expression, "the body I have," there is present a sense of possession, with a correlative sense of actual or possible alienation of my body from myself, who thus feels called upon to control it, that is absent from the expression, "the body I am." In the latter expression, there is not so much a suggestion of complete and undisputed possession as of a situation in which the question of possession, or its lack, does not arise. We can readily conceive of two types of situation in which such a question can be said not to arise. There is the case in which, so to speak, there is nothing but a body. To speak here of "having a body" would be to surreptitiously smuggle in the notion of a subject, not wholly identifiable with the body, who might lose control of it. Then, there is the case of an embodied subject for whom the question of mastery does not arise, precisely because his activity is an integrated functioning of his whole self. Now, while there are cases in which we experience such a situation or can witness its occurrence in others – we may think of the case of an ingrained habit, of a perfected skill, or of the ascetic grace of the saint – it might well seem to remain for most of us an ideal, rarely achieved and precariously maintained. On reflection, however, this is the truer the more intelligence and virtue are called into play in an activity. At the lower end of the scale, where activity is predominantly physical, there is a host of actions which we learn to perform with an ease born of functional integrity. This is especially true of that complex of organic activity, the process of learning which unfolds below the threshold of reflective awareness. It is equally true of actions which have been consciously learnt but whose continued and successful performance no longer requires our conscious attention. We are aware of "having a body," then, only when something occurs to disrupt this subliminal organization. Furthermore, the expression has meaning only for someone capable of taking conscious note of the disruption. This self-consciousness itself can, moreover, engender such a situation, as is the case when it hampers the graceful performance of a physical action: we are suddenly all fingers and thumbs.

The situation, therefore, expressed by the phrase "the body I have" is derivative and secondary. The primary situation is that expressed by the phrase "the body I am." This expression, however, can be ambiguous. It can evoke the pre-reflective situation in which the awareness has neither intruded to disrupt the style of embodied action nor yet taken note of its disruption. It can also refer to the situation in which reflection, having assumed its organic integrity, consciously moves towards the destiny of the integral self. It is here we can more truly speak of "the body I am," for as Marcel says "the experience of being is fulfilment."[1] What in fact this phenomenological analysis reveals in the situation of the embodied self is a duality of aspect.[2] There is an aspect of irreducibility and one of transcendence. The former is

---

[1] *M.E.* II, p. 46.

[2] Some qualification must be made in the use of the term "aspect" within the context of Marcel's philosophy. Strictly speaking, as Marcel remarks (Preface to *De l'Existence à l'Etre,* p. 13), "an aspect can only be seen." It thus belongs to the sphere of problematic distinction. There will, therefore, be a subtly different sense in the use of "aspect" in the context of problematic aspects, in the context of metaproblematic aspects, and in the context of a problematic contrasted with a metaproblematic aspect. In the latter case, Marcel would speak of the contrast between "an aspect and a non-aspect." *(loc. cit.).* The meaning of this distinction is exactly that of the distinction between the problematic and the meta-problematic. We shall continue to use the term "aspect" where necessary, without continually and tediously drawing the distinction. The meaning of an "aspect" that is strictly a "non-aspect" will become clear further on when we treat of the "non-specifiability" of the meta-problematic. That we are using "aspect" in this "non-objective" sense should be quite clear from the context in which we do use it.

perhaps more clear when we consider the pre-reflective experience of embodiment, where what invites recognition is the irreducible character of the embodied self. In the latter case, it is the orientation of the whole person towards his conscious integration – a movement transcending his emergent situation but which consciously assumes it in order to realize it more fully – that claims recognition. The transcendent aspect of the emergent situation itself is revealed in the experience of what Marcel terms "an exigency for being"[1] – a concept of great importance to the understanding of his thought, yet to be submitted to closer analysis. The point we wish to stress here is that the two aspects we have distinguished in the situation of the embodied self are both aspects of one and the same personal situation of which embodiment is an integral feature. A further point which should be remarked is that, if we take "having a body" to be an adequate description of the situation, those aspects will go unrecognized and the situation itself be misconstrued. In order so to describe it, however, we have adopted towards our embodiment an objective attitude that separates, while crystallizing the separation, our body from ourselves. It is in this sense that we can speak of there being operative a category mistake. It is a mistake precisely when we forget what limited scope there is for speaking of "a body," divorced from the self it embodies and with which it presents for a metaproblematic reflection an integral situation. Looked at in this light, the 'categories' of *being* and *having* coincide respectively with the *metaproblematic* and the *problematic*.[2]

We have earlier remarked the central rôle played by the concept of incarnation in Marcel's philosophy: "the existential point of view about reality cannot... be other than that of an incarnate personality."[3] Obviously, a philosophy that intends to give an adequate account of the person must deal satisfactorily with the relationship between that concept and the concept of embodiment. Such is the case above all, if one feels with Marcel that the concrete situation of being an embodied person is ill represented by any theory seeking to reduce it to one of being merely a body or by a theory that, in seeking to avoid such an unsatisfactory answer to the question, dissolves the situation into a relationship between two fully constituted objects as its mutually exclusive terms. This, rather than any question concerning the relation-

---

[1] C.f. *P.E.* p. 4; *M.E.* II. p. 39.
[2] *B.H.* p. 172. "It seems clear to me that the realm of having is identical with the realm of the problematic." For the identification of the realm of being with the metaproblematic, c.f. *op. cit.* pp. 170, 171.
[3] *B.H.* p. 10.

ship of mind and body, is the fundamental question in the ontology of the person. Since, on any account of the matter, both mental and corporeal activity are functions of the one subject, it seems reasonable to look for a solution of the latter problem within the framework of an answer to the question concerning the person's relationship with his own body. By placing the concept of embodiment within its appropriate setting at the point of divergence of the problematic and metaproblematic, on the frontier dividing the categories of being and having, Marcel not only shows how the answers he would reject could have been prompted by a false picture of the situation, engendered by the attitude he has diagnosed as objective. His diagnosis also points out the direction in which we should look for a more satisfactory answer. The situation of "having a body' is, we have remarked, secondary to and derivative of the situation of "being embodied" – an expression which covers the emergent and transcencent aspects of "being my body." The concept of embodiment, that is, as it functions in the category of having presupposes that concept as it functions in the category of being. In other words, more characteristic of Marcel, one can only speak of "having a body" against a background of "being embodied." We shall yet see, when we come to consider Marcel's own analysis of embodiment, his use of this principle to show that objectivity itself implies, phenomenologically and ontologically, the non-objective. The very ambiguity of the concept of embodiment, therefore, which seems to admit of translation equally by "*a* body" and by "*my* body," serves to make of it a key concept in the understanding of the concept of person. Thus, Marcel asserts that "incarnation" is "the central 'given' of metaphysic" – that is, of a philosophy whose focus is being: the metaproblematic – and also that "the setting-up of my body as the typical possession marks an essential stage in metaphysical thought."[1] Confronted with the problems involved in my thinking of my body as an object I possess, I am led to recognize equally the irreducible character of my embodiment and the transcendent character of my embodied self, together with the need to harmonize both features of my situation in my conception of what I am. It is precisely when I realize that the body as possession is a stage in philosophic reflection to be transcended that the path is open to an understanding of what I really am.

"I cannot concentrate my attention on what is properly called *my* body – as distinct from the body-as-object considered by the physiologists – without coming once more upon this almost impenetrable

---

[1] *B.H.* pp. 11, 163; on ambiguity c.f. *op. cit.*, pp. 156–157.

notion of having. And yet, can I, with real accuracy, say that my body is something which I have? In the first place, can my body as such be called a thing? If I treat it as a thing, what is this 'I' which so treats it? 'In the last analysis,' I wrote in the *Journal Métaphysique*, we end up with the formula: My body is (an object), I am – nothing."[1] The solution to this problem is, we have suggested, lies partly in a deeper understanding of what precisely is involved in the notion of having. It would be as well, therefore, to survey the main features of Marcel's analysis of that concept.

In analysing the concept of having, Marcel is not primarily intent upon exhibiting differences in our several uses of the word. His main concern is rather to focus attention upon a certain community of attitude informing those uses. To put it another way, the question is not merely one of distinguishing forms of speech, but of distinguishing subtle differences in attitude that betray themselves in distinctive styles of utterance and in differing styles of action. "What counts is not words, it is the inward attitude of which words are only the sign or symbol."[2] On the other hand, Marcel is not undertaking a purely psychological investigation. "The non-psychological character of such an inquiry as this," he asserts, "must be emphasized as strongly as possible; for it really concerns the contents of the thoughts which it is trying to bring out, so that they may expand in the light of reflection."[3] This is what Marcel understands by a phenomenological inquiry. It is a mode of inquiry whose subject is concrete experience, unprejudiced by problematic theorizing. For metaproblematic reflection, we may recall, the experiencing subject cannot be divorced from his experiencing without distortion of the situation under investigation and, consequently, prejudice to the outcome of the inquiry. Both the attitude adopted by the inquirer and the attitudes inherent in the situation into which he is inquiring are relevant to our understanding of any concept issuing from such an inquiry. This is particularly true of the concept of having, which like any concept relating to the person, must be referred to the situation that gives it meaning. The starting point for an investigation into that meaning, then, will not be a definition to be progressively explained so much as a human experience to be intensively explored. The experience, indeed, must be common, in the sense that appeal to it presupposes its potential presence in others. It need not be common

[1] *B.H.* p. 156; c.f. *J.M.* p. 252.
[2] *B.H.* p. 47.
[3] *B.H.* p. 158.

in the sense that it is its most trivial instance that should claim our attention. Words in common usage tend to be devalued and there are debased experiences as well as – indeed, as concomitant to – debased concepts. To really understand a concept, we must look to the relevant experience not at its least but at its most intense. While, therefore, Marcel would admit various extended uses of the verb "to have," he would nonetheless argue that any assertion about having derives, however deviously, from its use in a kind of prototypical statement where it is I who have. "It looks as if having is only felt in its full force and given its full weight, when it is within I have."[1] The paradign case is *my* having. This stress upon the person's involvement in the situation under investigation indicates the metaproblematic character of the inquiry.

Marcel distinguishes between having-as-possession and having-as-implication. It is clear, however, that he regards the latter as derivative from and as analogous to the former. The similarity linking the two uses of having lies precisely in the possessive attitude informing them. This attitude is properly the correlate of the situation that gives birth to the notion of having-as-possession. The question will arise, of course, whether the unconscious transference from the having of possession proper to that of implication – exemplified in such statements as "such-and-such a body has such-and-such properties" or "a certain geometrical figure has a certain property" – is in the last analysis justifiable. What, then, is involved in the notion of having-as-possession?[2]

In all having-as-possession we can discern a certain relationship obtaining between a certain *quid* – what is possessed – and a certain *qui* – "the centre of adherence or apprehension". The question is what is the nature of this relationship. Now, we can consider it formally or dynamically, distinguishing two aspects of it: one of reference, the other of appurtenance or appropriation. First of all, as Marcel quite rightly remarks, the *qui* is in some sense transcendent to the *quid*.[3] That is, there is a difference of degree or level between them, as clearly marked in such an instance as "I have my own ideas about that" as in "I have a bicycle." It is the dynamic aspect of the relationship, however, that gives its peculiar quality and significance to the more formal reference of the *quid* to the *qui*. The reference, in fact, derives from a claim of the *qui* to the *quid* and is expressive of a relationship that is *felt*. We stress this

---

[1] *B.H.* p. 159; c.f. *H.V.* p. 39.
[2] *B.H.* pp. 158, 160, 163.
[3] *B.H.* pp. 158-159.

feature of the relationship because it serves to bring out the peculiar
nature of the analysis which Marcel is conducting and the peculiar
nature of the concept issuing from such an analysis. It is what we might
term a situation analysis – though the use of the latter term can only
be provisional since, as we have seen, reflection is for Marcel recuperative
rather than analytic. Why this should be so and how we are to understand the kind of concept that is its correlative are questions to which we
shall yet return, for they intimately concern our understanding of the
concept of person in the context of Marcel's philosophy and his peculiar
contribution to the understanding of that concept as such.

We have already noted Marcel's remark that only in the paradigm
case of *my* having is having "felt in its full force." He goes on to say that
"if a 'you have' or a 'he has' is possible, it is only possible in virtue of a
kind of transference, and such a transference cannot be made without
losing something in the process." Again, he observes: "The statement
'I have' can only be made over against *another* which is felt to be other."
The *felt* quality of the relationship, which might pass unnoticed by a
purely formal analysis of the concept, or by one attending merely to
expressions of having in the second or third person, is more readily
apparent when we resort to the paradigm case of 'I have' and attend to
the situation of which it is the expression – that is, when possession is
literal or actual. In such a case there is introduced to our notice a further
feature of the experience of having, power: "power is something which
I experience by exercising or resisting it." It is, of course, possible to
try and sterilize the concept of having, to rid it of any dynamic significance. Such an attempt might be made by insisting that, even taken
in the sense of possession, having represents nothing more than the mere
fact of containing. Containing, however, cannot be defined in purely
spatial terms. "To contain is to enclose; but to enclose is to prevent,
to resist, and to oppose the tendency of the content towards spreading,
spilling out, and escaping." There is here also an element of power
that is clearly marked when having is conscious and, therefore, purpose-
ful. That is, the notion of having that would assimilate it to mere
containing, with the element of power or active enclosure all but
eliminated, is a pale derivative of the full-blooded concept. We may
remark that a similarly "unconscious transference," with "something
lost in the process," often occurs in the case of 'belonging.' In its strong
sense, belonging also involves control, which we are called on to
exercise either in the face of attempts to wrest from me what belongs
to me or in the face of its own attempts to elude my control. There is

no real sense, for instance, in saying that my dog belongs to me, if it totally ignores me, is in no way under my control, nor answers to my commands. The more formal or legal notion of ownership is merely a social recognition and license for the exercise of the right to control. The possession that is proverbially nine-tenths of the law is fundamentally a matter of control.[1]

The relationship expressed in terms of having is primordially a felt relationship. Having is radically a way of behaving towards... whose roots are in a prereflective affectivity of the *qui* and which betrays an underlying intentionality towards the *quid*. This means that the meaning of having cannot be disengaged by a purely linguistic analysis. Indeed, the use of the term will be more or less adequate in the measure that the fundamental attitude informing the genuine experience of having is present in the situation to which the concept is applied. It were beside the point, then, to argue that having has a different use when it is applied to money, material possessions, bodies, abilities, or properties. In so far as such instances are instances of having, the subject will betray the same fundamental attitude that is the dynamic aspect of the intentional structure of his relationship with the object possessed. "At the heart of having, then," Marcel asserts, "we can discern a kind of *suppressed dynamic*, and suppression is certainly the key-word here." Having, that is, unfolds a dialectic and "this dialectic has its spring in the tension without which *real having* does not and cannot exist."[2]

The tension that exists between the *qui* and the *quid* allows us to understand the real nature of their relationship. In the first place, having, while it *affects* the *qui*, cannot be reduced to a merely internal relation, for then it would be meaningless. In the second place, while the externality of the *quid* is a prime factor in the experience of tension, the tension itself is an effort to suppress that externality. Having, then, is found "in a scale where externality and internality can no longer be really separated." In the third place, having is incapable of resolving the tension which is its source and whose suppression is its fundamental purpose. This feature, in turn, points to the real nature of *desire*. "To desire is in a manner to have without having." The suffering that accompanies desire – most apparent when desire is in no way appeased or capable of appeasement, when it is pure desire – is "the friction of an untenable position." Furthermore, desire introduces us to the essentially temporal character of possession: its suffering issues from "the pain I

---

[1] *B.H.* pp. 159, 161. *M.E.* I. pp. 110–111.
[2] *B.H.* pp. 160–161, 164.

feel at the idea that I am going to lose what I have, what I thought I had, and what I have no longer." If, therefore, there is a two-fold permanency in having – that of the *qui* and that of the *quid* – this permanency is, of its very nature, threatened. "The threat is the hold exerted by the other *qua* other, the other which may be the world itself, and before which I so painfully feel that I am. I hug to myself this thing which may be torn from me, and I desperately try to incorporate it into myself, to form myself and it into a single and indissoluble complex." This struggle is hopeless. So long as the *quid* retains its otherness, it must remain a constant threat to the stability of the relationship which the *qui* is trying to establish. The relationship itself could only be stabilized through the *quid*'s and, consequently, its own extinction. This is manifest in the case of passion – as divorced from and, therefore, as caricature of love. Passion would reduce the person, its object – and precisely as object – to *quid*, that is, to the status of possessible thing. It is interesting to note the resemblance between passion, so conceived, and the relationship which Sartre deems to be that of love – a concept of love derived from his doctrine of the *en soi* and the *pour soi* which clearly pertains to what Marcel would call the category of having. Finally, the dialectic has another, its only alternative, issue in the alienation of the *qui* from itself in its absorption in the *quid*. "There is," says Marcel, "an irreversible progress from the *qui* towards the *quid*... The progress seems to be carried out by the *qui* itself: it seems to be within the *qui*." Unless I am indifferent to the fate of the object in my possession – in which case possession is merely nominal or residual – it is the centre of a whirlpool of fears and anxieties that tend to absorb me, with an intensity strictly proportionate to the strength of the desire that seeks to overcome the tension of having. "Having as such seems to have a tendency to destroy and lose itself in the very thing it began by possessing, but which now absorbs the master who thought he controlled it."[1]

As might be expected from the fact that having is primordially a felt relationship whose paradigm case is my having, its dialectic is most apparent in the case of my body, when this is treated as a possession. In this case, as religious asceticism has always recognized, the process of alienation is most marked. Not only is the care and comfort of my body the most constant source of the attachment binding me to the things which confront me in the world and which exert over me a power exactly proportionate to the strength of that attachment, but in itself my body can present the most tyrannical of all objects of attach-

[1] *B.H.* pp. 134, 160, 164; c.f. *P.I.* p. 136.

ment. Paradoxically, however, the stronger my attachment to my body, the nearer to extinction is my freedom and the less remains in me anything of real worth. "It seems that my body literally devours me, and it is the same with all the other possessions which are somehow attached to it... It seems that it is of the very nature of my body, or of my instruments in so far as I treat them as possessions, that they should tend to blot me out, although it is I who possess them." It might be objected that an instrument treated purely as an instrument – or, for that matter, when it is treated not as mere possession but as something to be used – could have no power over me, since I control it. Marcel answers with justice, that the objection overlooks the interval that separates control and use in which the object possessed finds play for its fascination, a danger made more intense by the very tension that exists in all real having. This abdication before the object of possession is the more inevitable, the more we are inert before objects themselves inert; it is the less inevitable, the more we are actively involved with something "that serves as subject-matter of a personal-creative act, a subject-matter perpetually renewed." In such a case, the object is no longer treated as a mere possession or as a purely external instrument. It becomes, as it were, both in intention and in act, a prolongation of my bodily powers, incorporated into my bodily presence in the world. It is, however, treated as an extension not of *a* body, but of *my* body, assumed by my active presence in the creative act. "In all these cases... having tends, not to be destroyed" – as would be the case with its extinction concomitant to the extinction of the *quid* – "but to be sublimated and changed into being." Correlatively, the process of alienation can issue only from an act of self-desertion: it is inaugurated, fostered and consummated by the abdication of my freedom in face of an object treated as object and by the betrayal of the responsibility which that freedom entails.[1]

It is now time to relate these reflections on having to the central question of the person and to consider their bearing upon our understanding of that concept. In the first place, the concept of having presupposes that of being. As Marcel says, "in order to *have* effectively, it is necessary to *be* in some degree, that is to say, in this case, to be immediately for one's-self, to feel one's-self, as it were, affected or modified."[2] The passage from 'I have' to 'I am' lies through my body, experienced, precisely, as mine. It is not merely that my body is the

[1] *B.H.* pp. 14, 164–5; *J.M.* p. 283; *P.I.* p. 184–5.
[2] *B.H.* p. 134.

constant reference point of "an unformulated assumption about where
I am in relation to other objects," nor that the position which I, and
therefore, my body occupies is "the base from which the sense of (my)
referring words and the sense of (my) actions are directed outwards."[1]
Behind the epistemological proto-fact that my situation as embodied
person constitutes "the presumed point of view from which all other
things are soon and interpreted," as behind the linguistic proto-fact
that my embodied self is, as reference-point, "a presupposition of the
use of language," lies the experience of myself as embodied. If, however,
as Marcel affirmed in the *Journal Métaphysique*, "every existent must
appear as prolonging my body in some direction or other," so that "in
this sense my body is at one and the same time the existent-type and in
a still deeper sense the reference-point for existents," it is precisely
"inasmuch as it is *mine*, that is to say inasmuch as it is non-objective."[2]
It is no mere coincidence that Marcel should speak of my body at one
time as *"le repère de l'Avoir"* and at another as *"le repère des existants."*[3]
The protofactual situation of my being embodied in a world is a felt
situation: that is to say, such a situation is pre-reflective not only in
the sense that it is a situation from which reflection must start but also
in the sense that it is a situation of which reflection must take account,
if it is to remain, as Marcel would say, "faithful to the real": "the world
exists in the measure in which I have relations with it that are of the
same type as my relations with my own body – that is to say, inasmuch
as I am *incarnate*."[4] There is a reciprocal influence of my attitude to my
body and of my attitude to the world, which results from the ambiguity
of my situation as embodied person – an ambiguity that is only the
notional transposition of an ambivalence of attitude. This ambivalence,
manifest in the tension characteristic of having, seems to lie at the very
points where the pre-reflective situation emerges into the fuller light
of reflective awareness. At this point of emergence, reflection is not yet
completely divorced from action, whose directive it immediately
supplies, nor thought yet securely insulated from feeling. Awareness
of self and of world has not resolved the ambiguity and the ambivalence
of their relationship, which appears as, at one and the same time, internal and external, is simultaneously felt to be one of sympathy and
antipathy together.

   Now, it might well be objected that to view the situation thus is to

---

[1] C.f. Hampshire, *op. cit.* pp. 79, 82.
[2] *J.M.* p. 261.
[3] *P.I.* p. 189; *J.M.* p. 261.
[4] *J.M.* p. 261.

view it in an emotional light and that this is something which a philosopher should avoid. The objection is worth some consideration, for 'emotive thinking' is an epithet likely to be applied to philosophies classified, somewhat loosely and inexactly we fear, as 'existentialist,' among which Marcel's is often listed, despite his rejection of the label, in our opinion, for good reasons.[1] Unfortunately, emotion' is a concept of varied interpretation whose exact meaning is a matter of controversy,[2] – nor is this the place to prolong it. At the root of the objection, however, there probably lies the feeling that to take note of the emotional colour of a situation as philosophically significant – something of which we should take account, if we are to arrive at a genuine understanding of the concept referring to the situation in question – is to somehow abandon 'objective thought' for merely 'subjective' and fanciful speculation. We have already given reasons for attending seriously to questions of attitude in the formulation or interpretation of concepts relating to the person as such. Further to this, it can be argued – as indeed it has been elsewhere[3] – that emotion or feeling is no more and no less subjective than thinking – in the sense that both are alike ascribable to subjects – and no less, nor no more, objective – in that both refer, each in its own fashion, to objects; that while each falls within the circle of a personal experience, either can be communicated to others, each have its symbolic and outward expression. If human behaviour be emotional as well as rational, both kinds are relevant to an inquiry into what it means to be a person and enter into an understanding of the concept we form of the person. Nor is it the case that emotional behaviour is always irrational or that rational, in the sense of reasonable and reasoned, conduct is completely unemotional. In the last analysis, the objection we have been considering seems to reduce to the simple assertion that reason as such is not emotion as such. This, however, provides no compelling reason for excluding the emotional aspect of the human situation from the field of philosophic inquiry or from the kind of evidence we may legitimately call upon in pursuit of it – unless, of course, such inquiry has been carefully so defined as to necessarily exclude it. There seems no good reason for doing so, nor is such the case with Marcel. Indeed, it is clearly his mind that the

[1] For Marcel's rejection of the "existentialist" label c.f. *M.E.*I. p. 5 and *J.M.* Eng. Trans. Preface, p. xii.
[2] C.f. James Hillman, *Emotion: a comprehensive phenomenology of theories and their meanings for therapy.* Routledge & Kegan Paul, 1960, for a comprehensive account of the various interpretations.
[3] John MacMurray, *The Self as Agent.* Faber, 1957, pp. 196–202.

demand for a stringently rational or objective approach to the question of the person rests upon an essentially static view of the concept that ill accords with the dynamic features of personal experience and which derives from an attitude of mind whose origin is itself emotional. What is important is the diagnosis of its origin, which Marcel locates in the ill-judged extension of the category of having to our conception of the relations existing between myself and my body, between my embodied self and the world.

By taking as paradigm case my self embodied in the world, we are enabled to assess the practical presuppositions and consequences of the theoretical attitude underlying and directing all thinking according to the category of having. In the first place, the theoretical attitude involv- ed in regarding my body as an object presupposes a practical decision to resolve the ambiguity inherent in a relationship felt as simultaneously internal and external by opting for its treatment and description as the former. For, having, as we have seen, while ultimately conceivable only within a situation that allows of such ambiguity, begins by regarding the object to be possessed as something external – though capable of being somehow incorporated into me – and proceeds to try and 'inter- nalize' my relationship with the object – though this relationship must still retain (*qua* possession of an object) something of its external quality. That is to say, whereas the felt relationship that is the concrete and pre- reflective basis of having is and must remain ambiguous, objective thinking rationalizes that relationship into a purely external one. In the second place, then, the objective attitude has practical consequences. In the case of my embodied self, these are, besides the ignoring of the original and irreducible nature of the relationship binding me to my body, the misrepresentation of that relationship either as being a juxtaposition of two discrete entities – which solution is quite unable to account for the felt quality of the actual relationship – or as being a *tertium quid* interposed between them. Should this latter be conceived of as something concrete, apart from the difficulty of providing a satis- factory explanation of what that might be, there recurs the problem of explaining the relationship between the *tertium quid* and the two (in effect) objects it is supposed to relate. Should the external relationship be taken in purely an abstract sense, it will in fact reduce to a sheer juxtaposition of its terms. Issue from the impasse might be sought in a denial of the reality of all but the physical term, objectified as the body. Mental experiences and, indeed, sensual or emotional experiences, insofar as they were not reduced to mere physical reactions, could then be allowed at best an epiphenomenal reality. As much as any idealist denial of matter in favour of mind, such a solution would beg the question, solving the problem only by prejudging any evidence that might be called in rebuttal.[1] Reflection upon the original and pre-predicative experience of being embodied – alike sensitive to the inherent ambiguity that the situation presents to reflection and critical of the latter's tendency towards an over-simplified resolution of the tension so engendered – leads to a recognition of an irreducible reality in the person of which physical and mental characteristics are aspects. We are still left, however, with the twofold question of the nature of that irreducible reality and of the nature of its relationship with these aspects. If we wish to avoid the inconvenience of postulating an unknowable substrate underlying visible properties or an ineffable noumenon lurking behind phenomena, physical or mental, we must prepare ourselves not only to allude to but even to talk about the self that exhibits such aspects, without converting self or aspects into objects or denying their distinction – however difficult it seems to express this clearly.

The whole point of Marcel's drawing a contrast between the category of having and that of being is to focus attention upon the irreducible character of personal reality. An inquiry, then, into the meaning of the concept of person cannot limit itself to the person either as logical or as epistemological subject – as purely formal condition of discourse or consciousness or in its rôle as basic particular in our conceptual scheme. Already in the Metaphysical Journal, Marcel had noted:

1. That the thing can never be regarded as a sum of predicates, for the plus sign only relates to the form of accumulation (the juxtaposition of interest), which is purely mental.
2. That the predicate only symbolises and determines an answer to a determined question, so that when we say A is p we merely mean that in function of the interest, A answers p.
3. That to ask oneself what A is, apart from the predicates, a, b, c, d, is either to ask what its other predicates are (which possibly has some meaning, whatever the predicates enumerated, for it may well be that an exhaustive enumeration is unthinkable) or else to ask oneself what A answers to a question which is not one of the thinkable questions, that is, to an absence of question. But we know that the answer is not precisely zero.

It is: *this*. A is a predicate (or a grouping of predicates) determined by the index *this*. And it is only this index that confers on A its apparent substantiality.

Thus we have no right to say that A can be reduced to a grouping of answers; the questions themselves are only possible on the basis of *this*, of immediate presentation.[2]

---

[1] Marcel specifically rejects ephiphenomenalism, as we shall see when we come to treat in detail of his analysis of embodiment.
[2] *J.M.* pp. 146–147.

Now, whatever we might think about the adequacy of these remarks as a logical account of subject-predicate statements, the point at issue is quite clear. It is not a question of formal logic at all, but a question concerning the existential pre-suppositions of any statement that is sensible and significant. (This is borne out by a footnote to the passage cited, wherein Marcel distinguishes between *judgments* bearing on *A* and those bearing on *an A*). It is a question of what it is that we refer to or describe when, in the context of the present inquiry, we refer to or describe a person. The inquiry is, as the evocation of 'being' to contrast with 'having' suggests, ontological. At least it is a distinct question to the logical one. And it could reasonably be regarded as a prior one – in what sense? in sense of importance: once it is settled what it is that we are talking about when we speak of the person, it will be time enough to consider what difference, if any, this fuller understanding of the concept might make to the logic of the predicative or referring use of expressions of which persons are the focus of application. That the ontological question is a reasonable one appears from the fact that all particular questions are raised in virtue of particular interests and that the person, even more than the thing, abides such questions. Though not yet formulated as such, the question implied as correlative to "the answer that is not precisely zero" anticipates the "total question" of metaproblematic inquiry – we recall that, for Marcel, to raise the ontological question is to raise the question of being as a whole and of oneself seen as a totality."[1] Similarly, the inquiry is distinct from – is in the same sense prior to and transcends the epistemological one: it is not the question of *how* do we know, so much as that of *what* there is to be known – again, we may recall that while "doubtless it is legitimate to establish certain distinctions within the unity of the being who thinks and who endeavours to *think himself*; ... it is only beyond such distinctions that the ontological problem can arise and it must relate to that being seen in his all-comprehensive unity."[2] That this latter question is a reasonable one receives a like justification in the epistemological to that which it received in the logical context: "being is what withstands... an exhaustive analysis bearing on the data of experience and aiming to reduce them step by step to elements increasingly devoid of intrinsic or significant value."[3]

We have seen that, for Marcel, predicates applied to a subject

[1] *P.E.* 7.
[2] *Ibid.*
[3] *P.E.* 5.

represent answers to determined questions raised in function of particular interests. This observation may help towards understanding the relevance of Marcel's analysis of having to the determination of the kind of question involved in asking what it means to be a person. It can also help us to see why, in fact, it is towards persons rather than towards things that he directs his metaproblematic inquiry. Now, it is clear that while predicates – and here one could as well say descriptions or pieces of information – considered precisely as answers to particular questions could be grouped in families and septs whose surnames were just those determinate interests in function of which they were framed, Marcel's grouping of questions into the contrasting categories of problematic and metaproblematic is not merely a prolongation of the former process. For all particular questions and their answers fall under the problematic category, while the metaproblematic, far from providing a convenient receptacle for still unformulated specialised questions together with their yet unproffered answers, comprises questions of a radically different kind involving a shift of attitude from just that which Marcel diagnoses as characteristic of having.[1] And it is this fact that can confound the issue; for, in one sense, it can be said that the metaproblematic is meta-categoric.' By this one would mean that being – in the present context, human being, the person *qua* person – was not a concept answering questions framed in function of particular or specialised interests. It is not the kind of thing, to use a Marcelian phrase, that can be effectively approached in a characterizing attitude.

Underlying our mental picture of things as subjects possessing characteristics, Marcel believes, there is a transference. This transference is of a possessive – fundamentally a felt – relationship to things and their characteristics, so that the things are no longer just spoken of but ontologically conceived as entities possessing properties. The thing tends to be pictured as something apart from the characteristics it has, while they tend to be pictured as discrete and separate entities – whether the thing be said to comprise properties, qualities or, in the case of conscious subjects, states. However determined the intention not to confuse the reality with the imaginative model, properties tend to solidify, subjects to vanish in a continual process of attenuation, until

---

[1] *B.H.* p. 151. "The order of having is the order of predication or the characterisable. But the metaphysical problem which faces us here is to what extent a genuine reality, a reality as such, lends itself to characterisation; and also whether being is not essentially uncharacterisable, though of course it will be understood that the uncharacterisable is not the same as the indeterminate."

we are left with a mere juxtaposition of characteristics. Yet the distinction between the thing and its characteristics is purely phenomenal. "The characteristic is picked out from others; but at the same time, we cannot say that the thing is a collection of characteristics." We can only juxtapose them, "if we ignore their specifying function and treat them as units or homogenous entities." To do so is to proceed upon an unwarranted metaphysical assumption. One may strictly treat as a collection a group of things, but not a thing as a collection of the characteristics by which we seek to specify what it is; for, as Marcel observes, "characteristics can only be asserted in an order that admits of the use of the word 'also.'" That is to say that characterisation as such presupposes the very reality to specify which is its function and presupposes it in such a way that its specifying process can in principle never be complete: reality is uncharacterisable."[1]

Such a pronouncement, Marcel admits is ambiguous and might well appear contradictory. He insists, however, that it be not taken as a confession of philosophical agnosticism. If there be an illusion in thinking that we can ever completely characterize things – that an exhaustive inventory of characteristics is possible – there is also an illusion in thinking that nothing more can be said about "what shows itself" – to use Wittgenstein's phrase – once all conceivable characterizing questions have been put and answered, or that such questions are the only meaningful ones. It is rather time to switch to another language game, played in a spirit very different from that informing those that belong to the characterizing family. Thus, Marcel defines his pronouncement upon the uncharacterizability of reality as meaning: "If I adopt the attitude to reality which all efforts to characterise it would presuppose, I at once cease to apprehend it *qua* reality."[2] The attitude in question is clearly the objective attitude informing problematic reflection. What identifies the latter and characterization is their "external" manner of proceeding:

In so far... as characterizing consists in enumerating properties, placing one beside the other, it is an absolutely external proceeding; it misleads us, and never, in any circumstances, gives us the least opportunity of reaching the heart of that reality which we are trying to characterise. But, speaking philosophically, the important point to recognise is that characterisation implies a certain setting of myself in front of the other and... a sort of radical banishment or cutting-off of me from it... by my implicitly coming to a *halt*, separating myself and treating myself (though I am not probably conscious of so doing) as a thing bounded by its outlines. It is only in relation

[2] *B.H.* p. 167–9.
[1] *B.H.* p. 168.

to this implicitly limited *thing* that I can place whatever I am trying to characterise. It is plain that the will to characterise implies, in the man who is exerting it, a belief at once sincere and illusory that he can make abstraction from himself *qua* himself.[1]

Characterization, then, while legitimate in its strictly specifying function, exercised as a function of a determined and particular interest, is illicit in any pretension it may have to giving an adequate, much less the only possible, account of what there is.

There are two distinct issues involved in this argument. First, as a pretension to giving an adequate entological account, characterization is "a claim to possess what cannot be possessed." In staking such a claim, one is being misled by a *model* – one's own "construction of a little abstract effigy" of reality. In approaching the ontological question, therefore, one must abandon any notion of intellection or reflection modelled, wittingly or unwittingly, upon *having*. It is much more an illumination or, from the subject's point of view, a recognition. "The closer we get to the topic of intellection properly so called, the more these metaphors centered on the acts of plucking, taking, or grasping, become really useless... To discover an intelligible relation... is not in any sense of the word to grasp something; it is really to be illuminated, or rather to have sudden access to some reality's revelation of itself to us."[2] True that, in the same place, Marcel would seem to allow the validity of the acquisitive figure when applied to "those acts of the mind which still partake of habit." There might seem to be a contradiction here of his strictures upon thinking according to the category of having. It would seem preferable to speak of habits as dispositions to behave in certain ways, provided they be understood to be the disposing of a subject: having presupposes being. There is a point, however, in recognizing that habits, in the sense of overtly active expressions of a subject's dispositions, can represent a certain rigidifying of his response to his situation in set patterns of behaviour. We could speak here of there being on his part a certain dimunition or withdrawal of his presence in that sector of his activity. This need not represent a total loss. The withdrawal may well be from the periphery of his field of activity in order to concentrate upon its focal point. A withdrawal from one sector may be required for its intensification upon another and, immediately or ultimately, more important one.[3] These considerations will recur later; here, they are relevant to the question of language as a medium of

[1] *B.H.* p. 108.
[2] *M.E.* I. p. 62.
[3] Such, for instance, is the idea underlying Christian asceticsm.

communicating experience. "If illumination is to be communicated," Marcel observes, "it must inevitably become language, and from the moment it has passed into a sentence it runs, in some degree, the risk of blinding itself and of sharing in the sad destiny of the sentence itself, which in the end will be repeated mechanically, without the person who repeats it any longer recognizing its meaning... This danger is not only one that attends a communication from myself to another person, but it also attends... a communication from me to myself."[1]

This brings us to the other issue involved in the argument about characterization. Language, in its ordinary use, equally with science, runs the perpetual risk of being exalted above its strictly specifying function. Since both are in a sense acquisitive systems, their discoveries, considered precisely as acquisitions, are easily presented as not only an adequate but even the only possible account of what there is. Far from providing such an account, if we accept Marcel's analysis, the acquisitions of science and language, considered as an acquired system of reference and description and in its mundane usage, represent answers to questions quite different in category to the ontological. Thought can indeed, he admits, "develop a system of taking its bearings by things, a system of increasing and even of infinite complexity: but its aim is to let the essence of things go."[2] Yet, that this question of the ontological remains over, above, and apart from those questions raised in function of the particular interests animating problematic inquiry appears from the very fact that all such inquiry either takes for granted or ignores the question of the integral reality which it is its function to specify. That a distinct mode of inquiry, the metaproblematic is both conceivable and, in principle, feasible appears once the strictly limited nature and purely specifying function of problematic inquiry is recognized.

The recognition that there is an ontological question of the person finally derives from the recognition of "the ambiguity of our condition which is that of a being involved in the world of things and who participates in it, but who on the other hand transcends that world and knows that he transcends it."[3] This ambiguous condition is precisely that

---

[1] *M.E.* I.p . 62.

[2] *B.H.* p. 169; c.f. *J.M.* p. 137ff.

[3] *P.I.* p. 191; c.f. Merleau-Ponty, *op. cit.* p. ii: "I am not the resultant or point of intersection o the manifold causalties that determine my body or my 'psychism'; I cannot think myself as a part of the world, as the simple object of biology, psychology and sociology, nor close in upon myself the world of science. Everything I know about the world, even through science, I know from a point of view that is mine or from an experience of the world without which the symbols of science could say nothing. The whole universe of science is constructed upon the lived world and if we would think science itself with rigour, exactly appreciate its sense and bearing, there must first be awakened that experience of the world of which it is the secondary expression."

revealed by the analysis of the paradigm case of having: the condition of being a human person embodied in a world. If from a position entrenched within the problematic, no other kind of philosophic inquiry than the problematic appears conceivable, nor any other kind of question than those falling within that category appears meaningful, it is because the "external" manner of proceeding native to it betrays an objective frame of mind that envisages the person in the manner of a thing isolated among things in the atomic world whose picture it characteristically projects. Reflection upon embodiment, the mode of our insertion into the world, on the other hand, reveals the objective view for a simplified interpretation of an ambiguous situation, itself the source of that tension which such interpretation attempts too simply to resolve. Certainly, there is no question of Marcel's sighing after a naive experience free of all interpretation. "The philosopher has by definitoin left behind him, as it were, a lost paradise... He cannot dream of going back below self-awareness; it is, then, on the contrary, through an effort to get beyond it that he can hope to re-establish the lines of communication that, somehow, have been blocked."[1] Self-awareness has here for Marcel the force of the English term self-consciousness in its colloquial use: it is, then, a product of sophistication to be tested by a more genuine wisdom. That is why Marcel asserts that his meta-problematic reflection is less concerned with immediate awareness than with the first mediations – interpretations, therefore, – through which such awareness is constituted as experience.[2] This is to say that ontological reflection is metaproblematic in two directions. It is at once phenomenological and hyperphenomenological. On the one hand, it must recollect the integral experience of being a human person, embodied therefore in the world, while remaining critically aware of the simplification of its original ambiguity through the sophisticated intervention of objective analysis. If one would speak of attending to appearances in this context, it would not be in the sense in which appearance is contrasted with reality: it is precisely to reality showing itself that we must attend, in which context the use of "appearance" is neutral with respect to any suggestion of merely "seeming." Meta-problematic reflection is hyper-phenomenological not only in the sense that the language in which it speaks is post-perceptual, but also in the sense that it seeks to speak not merely of our experience of reality but, through the reintegration and refining of that experience, of the reality

[1] *P.I.* p. 25.
[2] *P.I.* p. 20.

to whose presence it bears witness. Such an enterprise, then carries with it no denial of the independence of reality – in the obvious sense that we ourselves, other persons, the world of things exist whether we take thought of them or not. This does not mean, however, that such independence is absolute in the manner of the squat objectivity that problematic reflection tends to confer upon the things by which it takes its bearings. Nor does it mean that the sole type of relationship obtainable between the inhabitants of our world is that conceived in the objective terms of the problematic point of view.

This finally is the reason why ontological reflection is directed to the personal rather than to the impersonal reality of things. The existential crossroads of my world is my concrete situation of being embodied. This crossroads is the focus of a network of relationships which I entertain with myself and, through my embodied self, with the world. Significantly, my embodiment is the paradigm case of having; my body, the prototypical possession. The way I think of my relationship with my body influences my thinking about my relationship with the world. If my body be thought of as a thing, my relationship with the world can be conceived in no other terms than those of a thing among things. In such a context, my experience easily reduces to an awareness equally external with respect to myself as to the other objects by which it takes its bearings. It becomes objectively expressible in impersonal statements about those objects which, as points of reference basic to my conceptual scheme, stand at the limits of my language and my world. Strictly speaking, then, those points of reference, myself included, do not lie within my world, no more than their inward reality lies within the descriptive scope of my language. That language itself becomes a web of cross-references between topics, defined as focus of such references, themselves determined in function of the interests to which they answer. There would seem to be no more room here for a general concept of reality – which begins to look like an illusory topic of all topics – than for a general concept of the thing. Topics themselves dissolve into sub-systems of cross-references between sub-topics. Either world, the outer or the inner, reduces to an abstract structure whose skeleton takes on flesh only when the interest, to which topic and reference answer, has been defined. The question remains, however, in function of whom is the interest so defined and whence does it derive? In the language game, beside the board, the pieces, the moves, there is the mover; rules, even where most a matter of conventional agreement or of arbitrary choice, are in some measure determined by factors from outside the game; games are played by persons within a world.

On Marcel's analysis, any problematic game is played within a world – *my* world, in which I am involved and so involved because I am involved *with my* body, itself involved *with* the world. This *with* is in marked contrast to the *also* of characterization.[1] Here, the possessive relationship and the objective break down. I cannot, in the strict sense, be said to possess my body, nor am I linked to it as thing to thing. This is, as we have earlier seen, a matter of felt experience. It is pre-reflective, not in the sense – which would be a nonsense – that it eludes awareness, but in the sense that all consciously elaborated reflection must start from it, regard or disregard it. Objective reflection – Marcel's first reflection – disregards it. The idea of object and the idea of objective relationship, intercalated between objects, masks the felt experience of participation. In an objective world – in Marcel's meaning of the term – things are objects in function of my possessive or utilitarian interest, in function of my characterizing or classifying interest, or stand in external reference to their ontological selves on the periphery of the world defined by my objective interest. As co-participants, the inhabitants of the world in which I am are indeed distinct but not in objective fashion. They are really in relationship through their common participation in a common world. On the pre-reflective level, this participation is revealed through my receptivity. In that world, one would not speak of "the appearances of things" so much as of "things appearing," presenting themselves for my welcoming recognition. Since "experience functions as an idea" – in the context, an abstraction; extrapolated, an object – "once it is freed from the particular context that makes it mine,"[2] paradoxically, recognition of the other's *presence* can be realised only through the *recollection* of my own presence in the world: "the road leading to the other passes through my own depths."[3] That road, notwithstanding, is not purely introspective. The situation that reveals me as a presence irreducible in status to a mere object is a situation that reveals me as participant in a world. My presence in that world is intensified through my personal and conscious assumption of my relationship with its inhabitants. Recognition of the full meaning of my being a person must, then, embrace the possibilities of such growth in presence. It is true, nonetheless, that while conscious realisation of my felt participation in the world makes possible the recognition of a

---

[1] C.f. *J.M.* p. 169, 196; *B.H.* p. 168.
[2] *J.M.* p. 297.
[3] *P.I.* p. 25.

non-objective relationship with its inhabitants, this remains an impersonal relationship so long as it does not obtain between persons.
The essence of things, whatever that might be, eludes me. All that I
can attain is their meaning for me in function of whatever of my
interests they answer.[1] There is some importance, however, in recognizing that even with impersonal things there remains something beyond
those aspects they present to my reflection that eludes it. The temptation
to account myself an object among objects is lessened. The concept of
object is seen to be secondary and a derivative of my problematic
interests. I am reminded that essentially the world does not exist
merely for me, purely answering my purposes. To view the world in
this light is to look upon it as my home.[2] The sense of being at home in
the world might be deemed a mere poetic myth. The myth, however,
serves to sound the emotional resonance of metaproblematic reflection,
as alienation sounds that of problematic. If emotion be indeed the
symbolic apprehension of a situation, the myth serves a philosophic
purpose.[3] It so serves by keeping us in mind of the attitude involved in
recognizing my fundamental situation for what it is. Since it is only
from within that situation, consciously assumed that the world can
appear in some degree as it is, ontological reflection, *qua* metaproblematic, is directed towards the person rather than towards things. "A being
whose deepest reality consists perhaps not only in inquiring into the
nature of things, but also in questioning himself about his own essence,
is thereby situated beyond all the partial answers at which such an
inquiry can arrive."[4]

Even on this level, higher than the pre-reflective, ontological reflection escapes the kind of introspective prison that idealism tends to
construct. "To insist upon the non-objective character of presence is
by no means equivalent to saying that it is merely subjective. In reality,
it is of intersubjectivity that one must speak here."[5] It is not merely
that capacity for reflection and consequently for the conscious acceptance and assumption of one's situation betrays the presence in the world

---

[1] *H.P.* p. 52, where, speaking of 'designation' as 'a characterizing function,' Marcel
remarks that the notion that its essence "consists simply in the choice of a conventional sign
to serve as substitute for the thing designated... seems... to let escape the essential, inasmuch
precisely as this is non-functionalizable."

[2] C.f. *H.P.* p. 52–54.

[3] C.f. Hillman, *Emotion*, pp. 246–289, esp. pp. 264–6, 273–4.

[4] *H.P.* p. 73.

[5] *P.I.* p. 188; c.f. *U.A.* p. 7: "We must recognize that each of us, in order to realise what
may be called his own development, must open himself to diverse beings other than himself
and become capable of welcoming them without in any way allowing himself to be eclipsed
or neutralized."

of a kind of thing that is more than thing. The very condition of such a being betrays within him the need to develop through conscious commerce with fellows similarly endowed. Language itself, in which awareness of self and others must be expressed in order to develop, witnesses to this fact, especially if we regard it in its concrete manifestation as speech. Without worrying at this stage about the mediacy or immediacy of our awareness of other persons, we can recognize that the need for converse with other persons and the modes in which it develops are relevant to the understanding of the concept of person itself. Suffice it to remark that there is for Marcel a radical distinction between discourse in the third and discourse in the first and second person. While recalling much that has been already noted on the question of objectivity, the distinction throws some fresh light on what, in the Marcelian context, could be properly deemed a personal question. The essential concern of third person discourse is to furnish or procure information about an object of inquiry which, as such, readily appears as a "tabulation" of the information forthcoming. In such discourse, when a second person is addressed, it is in his function as "repertory" of the information sought. Certainly, statements in the second person aim at being heard but they are not directed to what is essentially personal in the person addressed. Even the question *who* asks or answers the questions is irrelevant to the validity of the statements made: this question is really that of credibility, raised only when the answer received is not the one expected. In the context of objective statements and of the kind of question designed to elicit them, there is no room for personalities. This is so, whether it be I or another who is either object of or party to the discourse. The other person only appears as *thou* – that is, as distinct from and other than "anyone at all" which is equivalently "nobody in particular" – when stress is placed not upon the information sought – about himself or anyone or anything else – but upon the idea of answering, which implies communion or 'us-ness'. This relationship, in appearance *dyadic* in contrast with the *triadic* relationship of objective discourse, is in reality an intentional identification: when we are two, we are in a certain manner only one. In other words, personal relationship and the personal discourse in which such relationship is expressed represent a conscious assumption and, therefore, a fuller realisation upon a higher level, of the felt participation in which my presence in the world is grounded. It involves then, whatever form it takes, an active reference to the personal reality of the other which lies beyond what is attainable in any objective description I can give of it – as does, indeed, my own personal reality for myself. The ultimate expression of this relationship is, of course, love or friendship. "The being I love is for me a *third person* in the least possible degree. Moreover, that being discovers me to myself, since the efficacy of his or her presence is such that I am less and less *him* for myself – my interior defences fall at the same time as the barriers separating me from somebody else. The being I love comes more and more into the circle in relation to which there are third parties, third parties who are the others." In love, the inadequacy of objective description with respect to the reality of the person loved is most manifest. It is a common experience that in its context epistemological questions of the kind that sometimes trouble philosphers lose their point. This does not mean that no objective description of another person is possible nor that it is for all purposes entirely useless. I can obviously learn a great deal about another person in this objective fashion. Although this is knowledge about him, however, it is not knowledge about him *qua* person. It only becomes such in the measure that it is subsumed under an intention towards him precisely as person. It is something like this that lies behind the religious injunction to love the sinner while hating the sin. Certainly, as far as objectively expressible characteristics go, one can have as clear a knowledge of a person's character in hating as in loving him. What is undeniably different in the two cases is that, when I love the evildoer, albeit detesting his deed, those facts appear in a quite different light. Through the recognition within him of a reality unexhausted by the objectively stateable facts, a real hope arises of his redeeming himself or of his being redeemed – a hope which alone can initiate any co-operation in that work of redemption. The recognition, then, has practical bearing upon the question of my behaviour towards others. This recognition of the person *qua* person should not be confused with "acquaintance with" evoked in contrast to "knowledge about." That dichotomy belongs to the field of objective reflection. Just as "acquaintance with" changes its index once its intention is directed towards the person recognized as person, so also does "knowledge about." That is to say, while metaproblematic reflection is quite distinct in its intentional structure to problematic reflection, this latter can serve the kind of activity initiated by the former, though in a subordinate capacity. To put it in other terms: problematic awareness of persons – knowledge about or acquaintance with objects that happen to be persons – is personal *per accidens*; metaproblematic awareness of persons is personal *per se*. The *per accidens* and the *per se*, derive from the intentional attitude informing either reflection.

This distinction of attitude, however, is not philosophically trivial; it enlightens us as to what it is we seek to be aware of in either case.[1]

This reality of the person *qua* person, which lies beyond all partial replies expressed in objective statements and which is envisaged even by someone accepting their validity, inasmuch as the subject to which they are referred is a *thou* for him, is the subject of an ontological inquiry into the identity of the person. To ask "who or what you are" in this sense is to ask a question similar in kind and category to "who or what am I." To see the question for what it really is, to envisage what kind of answer is really required by such a question, demands of the inquirer the adoption of a similar attitude in either case towards the subject of his inquiry. Certain kinds of answer have already been in principle ruled out as inadequate or nonsignificant. The answer, for instance, will not lie in any reduction of the concept of person to that of a collection of states or in its substitution by the notion of an instantiation of predicates. In the first case, apart from difficulties posed by Hume's position noted by contemporary philosophers[2] as well as the difficulty of deciding the nature of the relationship that connects the distinct states – apart also from the unconsidered difficulty of defining within the topic of the self the sub-topic of the state, whose identity is required for an objective relationship between states to have meaning – it is clear that in this context the question of the person, as Marcel's conceives it, cannot even begin to be raised. Whatever that self is, it is not the person. In the second case, the question is merely transposed into linguistic terms. The limitations of such treatment of the person have already been noted, together with the essential inadequacy of any answer it can provide. It points in the right direction, if it be taken to mean that the concept of person is a basic particular to which reference is made in our conceptual scheme. Indeed, Marcel's removal of the concept of person from the category of having can be said to have something in common both with no-ownership doctrines of the self and with their rejection. In the first place, he would seem to agree that ownership, in the sense of and as necessarily implying possession, is not the kind of relationship that obtains between me and what can be picked out as my characteristics: he would, however, extend this objection to include my body

---

[1] *J.M.* pp. 137–140, 157–7, 196, 293; c.f. John MacMurray. *Persons in Relation.* Faber, 1961, p. 170, where will be found a similar view of "knowledge through hatred."

[2] C.f. A. J. Ayer, *The Problem of Knowledge.* Pelican, 1956, pp. 191–192, 198; A. H. Basson, *David Hume.* Pelican, 1958, pp. 131–132; P. F. Strawson, *Individuals.* Methuen, 1959, p. 103; C. H. Campbell, *On Selfhood and Godhood.* Allen & Unwin, 1957, pp. 78–79; S. Hampshire, *Thought and Action.* Chatto & Windus, 1960, pp. 126-127.

or anything of which it is comprised. In the second place, he could well
agree that the predicative "to be" is not a relational verb like "to
possess," but would insist on our keeping well in mind the purely
specifying function of the latter in its objective use, while probably
remarking that to speak of "non-transferable ownership" in the context
is not properly to speak of ownership at all. Certainly, there is a relationship between the person and what is attributed to him: it is not, however,
an objective one and where we must speak of relationship, participation
is a better word for it. It is a step forward to recognize that the concept
of person is primitive: that is, that it is logically prior to the concept of
an individual consciousness. We must add, however, in the light of
Marcel's analysis of having, that is equally prior to the concept of an
individual human body. We may concede, then, that the concept is
not to be analysed as that of an animated body or of an embodied
anima, if by 'anima' be understood the concept of mind or individual
consciousness. For both the concept of 'individual consciousness' and
that of 'individual body' are derivative and secondary to the concept
of person. It is as well to remark, nonetheless, that this does not dispose
of the concept of soul, which is not identical with that of mind. Arguments that the mind is merely the topic of mental behaviour or, alterna-
tively, of dispositions to behave in a certain way that can be characterized as intelligent, or, again, a complex of both – while they might
conceivably dispose of the mind as substrate to acts or dispositions or of
the mind erected into an entity in itself – do not dispose of my soul as
a reality, one moreover capable of surviving the dissolution of the link
uniting my soul with what *was* my body in one person, myself. Nor do
such arguments dispose of the person as an integral reality which
corporeal and spirutual characteristics simply specify and, specifying,
presuppose. This is not yet to assert anything about the possibility of
survival nor of what is to be understood by my soul. It merely points to
a difference, too often ignored, between the concept of mind and that
of soul, between the concept of person and those of mind and body. It
is also clear that the concept of person is not that of ego, empirical or
transcendental: both are essentially abstract notions, the one abstracting
from the person what is objectively stateable, the other the unstateable
residue, whereas what exists is "the real individual that I am, with the
incredibly minute detail of his experience, with all the specifications of
the concrete adventure that belongs to him alone to live, to him alone
and to no one else."[1] The mere acceptance, then of persons as primary

[1] *H.V.* p. 191.

particulars basic to our conceptual scheme, even in their function as common focus of corporeal and mental attributes, says nothing of what it means to be a person. It points to the subject of inquiry; it does not yet give us the sense, as distinct from the significance, of the concept. Neither, by denying that the human person is a composite of two substances, *a* mind plus *a* body – that he is a ghost in a machine –, does it follow that he might not be both embodied and spiritual. Much less has a beginning been made in the consideration of what this might mean.

The question of the meaning of the concept of person, then, is identically the question of who I am. To ask it in general is to ask what it means with reference to any given person. Asking it of any other person, however, if I am to see what the question means and what kind of an answer is required, involves asking it of him as I would of myself. Such a question, therefore, is not a problem. "Where a problem is found, I am working upon data placed before me; but at the same time, the general state of affairs authorises me to carry on as if I had no need to trouble myself with this Me who is at work: he is here simply presupposed." When the person is subject of inquiry, however, the presupposed is in question. The 'problem' of the person is one "which encroaches upon its own data and invades them, and so is transcended *qua* problem." It is in this sense that the question of the person is a question of being. "When the inquiry is about Being... the ontological status of the questioner becomes of the highest importance. Could it be said, then that I am involving myself in a infinite regress? No, for by the very act of so conceiving the regress, I am placing myself above it, I am recognising that the whole reflective process remains within a certain assertion of what I *am* – rather than *which I pronounce* – an assertion of which I am the place, and not the subject. Thereby we advance into the realm of the metaproblematic."[1] The question of Being and of my being, whatever the distinction or relationship between them, find a common focus in myself as person. The question of my being is the question of my being in its entirety and only by considering this question can we come to understand what the question of being might be. The concept of person, that is, is fundamental to a concrete ontology, If reflection upon the person is ontological in this sense, it is "an ontology that proceeds by way of concrete approaches." That is, it is not so much a matter of intuition as a search for an intuition: by means of which "thought *stretches out* towards the recovery of an intuition which otherwise loses itself in proportion as it is exercised." If it is an intuition, it is

---

[1] *B.H.* pp. 170–171; *P.E.* pp. 7–8.

"an intuition which cannot be, strictly speaking, self-conscious and which can grasp itself only through modes of experience in which its image is reflected and which it light up by being thus reflected in them." If it is a reflective process, then, it is not a withdrawal from experience. To reflect ontologically is not "to mirror oneself in the intelligible unity of subject and object," a dichotomy that belongs to the sphere of problematic reflection. The process is *recollective*: "No ontology... is possible except to a being who is capable of recollecting himself... The word means what is says – the act whereby I re-collect myself as a unity." This recollection is not just an initial moment preliminary to ontological reflection but the attitude which makes such reflection possible and within which it unfolds: "it is within recollection that I take up my position-or, rather, become capable of taking up my position – in regard to my life." As such, it defines the essential difference between an onlooker's view of experience – detached, uncommitted, uninvolved – and a participant's, which is contemplative: "There can be no contemplation without a kind of inward regrouping of one's resources, or a kind of ingatheredness; to contemplate is to ingather oneself in the presence of whatever is being contemplated, and this in such a fashion that the reality, confronting which one ingathers oneself, itself becomes a factor in the ingathering." Recollection, in fact, involves my conscious assumption of my participation in the world. It does not therefore, imply any relaxation of the ontic and intersubjective bonds binding me to the world. It does, however, make possible the understanding of the fundamental orientation of my being as a whole which receives only partial expression in my life, considered in contra-distinction to myself as an actualization of my potential development as a person: "*in this withdrawal I carry with me that which I am and which perhaps my life is not.*"[1]

'Orientation' recalls other words of the same family already used in the elaboration of the distinction between the problematic and the metaproblematic, such as 'attitude,' 'direction,' 'intention.' These words can have different connations in the differing contexts of their ordinary use. In the present context they occur because they refer to a situation that is always developing: for the person, we recall, to be in situation and to be on the move are two aspects of the same condition.

---

[1] *P.E.* pp. 12–14; *M.E.* I. pp. 144–145. Here will be noticed a divergence in our interpretation of Marcel's ontologico-phenomenological method from that given by Professor Ian Alexander. C.f. *Actes du Premier Colloque de la Société Britannique de Philosophie de Langue Française.* Londres, 1962, pp. 7–8. We cannot quite accept his interpretation of Marcel's "recollection." C.f. further below, p. 95.

'Fundamental' recalls that the context is metaproblematic: it is not just a question, therefore, of a particular intention, no more than it could be a question of a particular interest, a determined question, a specific answer, an objective description. The term also reminds us that it cannot be purely a subjective affair nor merely a matter of conscious personal decision. One might say that it signified a dynamic *a priori*, in the sense that it was not innate, – meaning thereby that while its presence could be recognized by everyone, granted the good will and the unprejudiced mind, it would not necessarily be so recognized without that recognition's being consciously sought or even awakened by some prompting. If it be an *a priori*, it will not be one deducible by mere abstract reasoning, divorced from concrete experience. It is an intention inherent in personal experience, recognized in its actual experiencing. The term best suited to signify this 'fundamental orientation might well be Marcel's own term, '*exigency*.' "The exigency of being is not a simple desire or a vague aspiration," he asserts. "It is, rather, a deep-rooted interior urge, and it might equally well be interpreted as an appeal."[1] Exigency is not desire; for this belongs to the problematic and is a modality of having. It is not simple need; for the exigency is not for something *wanted* but for something *demanded* by the very constitution of my personal and ontological reality. "The exigency... is in me."[2] *Without* it I would not be what I *am*. It is the presence of this exigency that transforms awareness of the mere linguistic fact that all specifying expressions presuppose, if significant, the reality they specify into the recognition that all reflection takes place within the affirmation of being – an affirmation that eludes all attempts to objectivize and adequately to symbolize it.[3] The exigency, moreover, is present not only as the dynamic aspect of affirmation but appears in appropriate guise at every level of personal experience: thus, and precisely from this point of view, "I am present to myself as embodying certain values or, at least, as nourishing certain exigencies.[4] Exigency, therefore, includes an effective aspect that might well escape notice in the substitution for it of the term, 'intention.' "Is not that which has value," asked Marcel, "that which increases in me the feeling of presence?"[5] This does not mean that affectivity takes over the role of intelligence in Marcel's philosophy. "Feeling, after all," he writes, "is

---

[1] *M.E.* II. p. 39.
[2] *Ibid.*
[3] C.f. *P.E.* p. 7–8; *B.H.* pp. 27, 30, 31, 37, 38, 59.
[4] *P.I.* p. 143.
[5] *J.M.* p. 306.

only the sum total of the relatively disconnected phrases through which
the idea passes in order to take cognizance of itself, in order to be able
to formulate itself as idea."[1] The last phrase quoted could be misleading. It probably derives its somewhat consciously intellectualist
tone from the passage cited from Hocking upon which it closely follows.
Not that exigency should be given an anti-intellectualist interpretation,
but that Marcel's philosophy accommodates feeling more intelligently
than a problematic and rationalist philosophy can. His metaproblematic
conception of the person invites a more integral understanding of
experience in which affectivity and intelligence play an equally effective
role, receptive and communicative, in the integral experience of the
person who integrally experiences his situation. The idea, in fact, is
experience become fully presence, presence fulfilled. "Being is expectation made good, the experience of being is fulfilment."[2] Since fulfilment of being is a personal fulfilment – of the person in his integral
reality – the exigency for that fulfilment is an exigency of the integral
person, of his whole being. Thus, exigency and fulfilment alike involve
the person as a "situated" participant in the world, through the developing intensity of his presence in that world, to his fulfilment as a
truly personal being, a presence at once fully subjective and fully
intersubjective: "fulfilment is interiorized as soon as we enter the
domain of either personal or inter-personal intersubjectivity."[3] This
involves a fresh notion of activity. No longer conceived in the problematic terms of productivity – the fashioning of something extrinsic to
oneself – activity, metaproblematically conceived, becomes creativity,
allowing room for the recognition of a purely spiritual domain of
activity and ontological fulfilment none the less, perhaps the more, real
and "intersubjective" for that. "I think we must all, in the course of our
lives, have known beings who were essentially creators; by the radiance
and love shining from their being, they add a positive contribution to
the invisible work which gives the human adventure the only meaning
which can justify it. Only the blind may say with a sneer that they have
produced nothing."[4] An examination of the themes of invocation – as
Marcel designates the strictly personal encounter – that is, of fidelity,
belief, hope, and love, will clarify his conception of personal and
creative activity. These, as we shall see, are the essential modes in

[1] *M.E.* II. pp. 42–43.
[2] *M.E.* II. p. 46 (for the existential unity of the affective and cognitive aspects of human
consciousness, c.f. Chapter 2).
[3] *Ibid.*
[4] *Ibid.*

which personal freedom is expressed – a freedom that, as metaproblematic, transcends the objective categories of the determined and undetermined. The fact that Marcel allows of exigency being interpreted as "appeal," marks the fact that his philosophy, as one whose central concern is with the person, is in this sense a philosophy centred on freedom.[1] Since this is so, the recognition of the exigency that orientates that freedom is itself free. Since personal reality as such transcends the problematic and with respect to any problematic inquiry directed to what happens to be a person stands at its limit, it is always possible, by maintaining the problematic attitude and its objective point of view, to miscognize the reality in question and to assert, since the concept cannot adequately or fully be expressed in problematic terms, that there is nothing that can meaningfully be said of it. If the evidence called in defence of the metaproblematic concept of the person is by way of appeal to common experience, we must remember the strict sense, previously defined, in which it can be said to be common. The experience may be had, while its meaning is missed. It is partly in order to awaken recognition of its metaproblematic meaning, partly in order to deepen that recognition once awakened, that Marcel insists upon tackling question like that of the person by way of "concrete approaches." What follows, then, will be in part by way of confirming, partly by way of filling in, the outline already sketched.

Before passing to the consideration and evaluation of those concrete approaches, something might be said of the "kind of concept" involved in this inquiry. Marcel, in recent years, has been at some pains to dispel the impression that he is an "anti-conceptualist" thinker. "There is not *and has never been* in my mind any question of under-estimating the role of the concept in philosophy. But what has always appeared to me extremely suspect is the abstract representation and configuration of the concept with which the mind seeks to provide itself... The genuine concept, in the very measure in which it is that by means of which one thinks, is essentially reluctant to becoming something which the mind places in front of itself in order to dismantle it. This operation is only licit in the measure in which it is completed by a second reflection that allows of discerning what is illicit in it, or at least deeply deceptive... In its heuristic usage, concept should be identified with idea inasmuch as this latter is itself dynamically interpreted."[2] Marcel is here quite obviously distinguishing between problematic and metaproblematic

---

[1] *P.I.* p. 19.
[2] Communication to the "Réunion sur la Phénoménologie." C.C.I.F-20. ii. 1952.

concepts. The problematic "object" is something I confront with complete detachment, while metaproblematic "presence" is an experience in which I am inextricably involved. So too, while the problematic concept may specify some or other aspect of a subject or serve to indicate that subject himself – yet objectively and in some sense apart from those aspects, so that the meaning of such a concept in its referring use can readily reduce to the rules that govern its correct employment, – the metaproblematic concept of the person refers to a subject integrally – not indeed as the mere product of his experience, but as one whose integral reality is created through his conscious appropriation of his given circumstances. For, the person, metaproblematically conceived is such that the data of his experience – which considered in abstraction from their active appropriation by him appear to be contingent – are not contingent, thus appropriated, and cease to appear so, once thus considered.[1]

Now, obviously, the concept cannot be taken to actually include in its intension, except perhaps in its application to a given person, the particular experience that is his. The point is rather that the concept of person, even in its universal sense, includes in its intension this power of appropriation and, therefore, the essential modes in which such appropriation can be effected. This is indicated by saying that the concept is to be interpreted dynamically. It is dynamic in the correlative sense that the situation from which it derives is a developing situation. And this, after all, corresponds to a feature of words in their concrete us in living speech: there, their meaning develops in intensity with deepening experience. The heuristic character of such a concept draws attention to two aspects of its universality. In its universal use, it may be taken to intend the typical or the ideal. As intending the typical, the concept defines the minimum conditions that must be fulfilled by any particular to be included within its extension. As intending the ideal, the concept indicates the ultimate ontological fulfilment of the person *qua* person, though not as an ideal that will ever be, in fact, completely realised by any given person. Both aspects are involved in the universal scope of the concept: the ideal, insofar as it represents the potential achievement towards which the person as such is radically orientated; the typical, insofar as any given person must represent in some degree a realisation of the ideal. These twin universal aspects of the concept are, then, correlative and correspond with thos twin aspects, the irreducible and the transcendent, which, Marcel says, go far towards defining

[1] *M.E.* I. pp. 149–151.

"man's metaphysical condition."[1] Both aspects, too, come into play in
the particular application of the concept, for the individual person in
his irreducible reality is transcendentally orientated towards his
ontological fulfilment. That is to say, his "thisness" – being *this* person
– and his "thusness" – being this *person* – evolve reciprocally: being
most fully person, he is most truly human and most completely himself.
We might say, then, that the concept is ambivalent, though consistently,
or analogous, and that intrinsically. This feature of the concept corresponds to the varying intensity possible to presence, itself a feature of
our experience.[2] The dynamic interpretation and heuristic use of the
metaproblamatic concept of the person marks it as what Marcel would
call *"une idée profonde"*: an idea in which the now and then, the near and
far, meet or, rather, in which such opposition is transcended; an idea
which is essentially that of a promise to be fulfilled: "an idea presents
itself as profound in the measure that it opens out into a beyond that is
only glimpsed."[3] The sense in which the person, who is fundamentally
"situated in the world," can be said to transcend the spatial and temporal
aspects of his situation, we have yet to examine. The *"idée profonde,"*
however, corresponds with that ambiguity of our condition as "a being
involved in the world of things and who participates in it, but who on
the other hand transcends that world and knows that he transcends it."

Finally, the concept of person may be said to be an "integrator"
concept, not merely in the sense that it is the common focus of attribution
for all specific and specifying descriptions of the person but in the sense
that the relevance of such specifications is clarified in the light of our
understanding of what kind of concept that of the person is. Recognition
of the fundamental and ontological exigency of the person, involved in
the recognition of the dynamic character of the concept, provides a
principle of integrating all the various particular intentions of the person
which are manifestations of the fundamental exigency on varying levels
of experience. The intergration is not only vertical, but horizontal too:
for presence develops not only internally but through the presence of
the person to and with other persons. This integrative recognition,
Marcel terms *synidesis*. "Person – involvement – community – reality:
here we have a chain of notions, not strictly deducible from each other...
but capable of being grasped in their unity by an act of the mind which
is fittingly described, not by the sullied term of intuition, but the too

[1] *B.H.* p. 157.
[2] *P.I.* pp. 114, 155, 160.
[3] *M.E.* I. p. 208 (author's translation), c.f. *ibid.* pp. 208–211 and *P.I.* pp. 29–35.

little used one of *synidesis*, the act by which an *ensemble* is maintained under the mind's regard."[1] We might call it a knowledge through convergence of aspects rather than by juxtaposition of properties. Synidesis is not an analytic process developing by way of abstraction from a sum of juxtaposed properties towards the definition of a general characteristic common to them all and which can then be adequately enshrined within a strictly univocal concept. As the sweeping glance that comprehends the smile that lights the human face without fixing upon the separate detail of each feature, synidesic reflection holds in focus a concrete unity recognised in the integral presence of the person and in which its several aspects fuse. In this process, aspects play the rôle not of material for abstraction but of concrete conditions for a recognition that can operate – as well in the case of other persons as in my own case – immediately or after more or less prolonged reflection. The recognition, moreover depends as much upon the subject reflecting – his attitude and consequent aptitude – as upon the subject of reflection – whose rôle is directly relevant perhaps, only to forming the concept of a given individual person. The organizing principle of the synidesis of metaproblematic reflection is the fundamental ontological tendency of the person as such, whether recognized as exigency or intention, that is never adequately formulated nor yet complete formulable, but which defines the universal scope within which fall the particular intentions of the person towards the specific goals accessible to him. In the synidesic concept, therefore, value and being coincide, for it is the concept of a being whose fundamental and irreducible reality is transcendentally orientated towards an ontological ideal. "Considering matters no longer from without but on the contrary from within, from the point of view of the person himself, it does not seem as if he can strictly assert of himself: I am, He grasps himself much less as being than as will to transcend what all at once he is and is not, an actuality in which he feels himself in truth engaged or involved, but which does not satisfy him: which is not up to the aspiration with which he identifies himself. His device is not *sum*, but *sursum*."[2] The isolation of ought and is belongs to the problematic. If the experience of being is fulfilment, its recognition is at once cognitive and affective. The ontological itself, moreover, no longer stands at the limits of experience but is within it as its dynamic principle. Though not objectifiable, the ontological structure of the person is manifest in his several aspects, held in synidesis, just as his

---

[1] *H.V.* p. 27.
[2] *H.V.* p. 32. For qualifications in the use of 'aspect', c.f. note 2, p. 25, *supra.*

physical aspect or behaviour acts not as intermediary but as vehicle of his presence. The concept of person, therefore, cannot be thought of as an object interposed between me and what I experience. It is not a medium *in* which reality is pictured or *from* which it is inferred but *through* which a presence is recognized and held in sharpening focus. It is in this sense that it can be said to be identified with idea. It is not idea – insofar as idea speaks complete coincidence of presence – no more than the reflection in which it evolves is intuition. But insofar as the metaproblematically reflecting mind can be said to be a faculty in quest of its intuition, the concept in which it integrates its experience can be said to be a concept evolving towards idea. "Naturally, there is no possibility of doing without symbols; nevertheless symbols should always be recognized as such and should never encroach on the ideas that one is straining to elucidate."[1] The word as sign must abdicate in favour of the word as symbol; the concept as symbol, in favour of the idea in the measure that it is presence recognized and enjoyed.

The complex meaning of the metaproblematic concept of person must be explored on the varying levels of experience on which is manifest the presence it intends. We must, then, direct our inquiry to the person as manifest at either limit of the scope of problematic reflection, a presence at once irreducible and transcendent. This means that we must inquire into the nature of his existential situation – existent and embodied – and into the manner of his emergence from that level of "submerged participation" into the conscious community of being – as a person in communion with other persons. This latter part of the inquiry will be concerned with the themes of what Marcel terms "invocation": fidelity, hope, belief and love. In elucidating these notions, we shall be clarifying the scope and content of the concept of person in the philosophy of Gabriel Marcel.

[1] *M.E.* I. p. 56.

CHAPTER III

THE EXISTENTIAL SITUATION

"The existential point of view about reality cannot be other than that of incarnate personality."[1] The concept of existence in Marcel's philosophy derives its significance from the metraproblematic context of the personal situation in which it is properly evoked. Viewed within that context, the concept manifests a concrete character denied it when viewed in abstract isolation from the situation to which it fundamentally refers. In Marcel's opinion, the profound justification of the philosophies of existence has been to stress the impossibility of not taking into account, when considering an existing being, its mode of existing. Without necessarily positing the priority of existence to essence, they bring to light the misconception involved in representing the relationship between essence and existence as an inexplicable and adventitious addition of the latter to "an essence already sufficient unto itself."[2] Marcel clearly recognizes that the existential question does not arise in the same terms for things and being: there is a radical distinction between existing impersonally and existing personally. If the question, at first sight, appears less acute with reference to things – and, here we may interpolate, for persons insofar as they are treated as things –, in their regard we know less what existing might be. "'There exists' is said about something for which it is intended to propose a definition or the beginnings of a definition: there exists a country where... Stress is not placed upon its uniqueness, rather the reverse. On the contrary, existence in the personal sense implies ipseity, reference to lived actuality."[3]

This line of argument clearly points in the direction taken by Marcel's analysis of the specifying function of characterization, with its attendant recognition of the uncharacterizability of the integral reality specified. Reality was said to be uncharacterizable, we may recall, not in the sense that the characterizing process as such was illicit, nor in the sense

---

[1] *B.H.* p. 10; c.f. *H.C.H.* p. 196: "from the point of view of man – and that is a pleonasm. for there is only a point of view from man and starting from man."
[2] *H.P.* pp. 20–21.
[3] *P.I.* pp. 149, 169, 170.

that there lurked beneath the characterizable properties an unknowable substrate, nor even in the sense that there must always remain an uncharacterized residue yet to be characterized. The point made was that the focus of individuality, the ipseity, reference to which lent significance to and was presupposed by the characterizing process lay beyond the scope of that process. The legitimacy of the latter was restricted to its properly specifying function, operable in virtue of strictly determined interests to which the object of inquiry would be made to answer. Within such a process, the existential question as such could not arise. At most, its possibility could be alluded to as that of a limiting question arising on the boundaries of the system defined by the strictly limited scope of problematic inquiry. The legitimacy of the question, then, it is outside the scope of such a system to determine. In this, the existential is like the ontological question. Thus, while Marcel concedes that the existence of things is not offered or proposed to us merely as a spectacle, this is so because we have concrete experience of their resisting us. Such an awareness, however, is clearly extrinsic. It can be deepened through recognition of our pre-reflective participation in a common world. As pre-reflective, both participation and awareness occur not as isolated experiences but as integrated aspects – noematic and noetic – of an integral and personal experience that resumes them in its conscious evolution. Reflection can, indeed, recognise or ignore the pre-reflective structure of experience, as it can accept or reject the existential exigencies this reveals. Ignorance and rejection, however, are alike arbitrary, since they can be justified only by a deliberate restriction of what is to count as significant experience. Furthermore, the proper context of the concept of existing would appear to be that of the more comprehensive concept of person; for, as we have already noted, the concept of person is prior to either that of body or that of mind, themselves the specifications of the integral reality that is base of the concept of person. It is, as Marcel asserts, in relation to my body that all other existents are affirmed.[1] This is not so, as we shall see confirmed, in the sense that my embodiment is a fact from which may be inferred the existence of other bodies. My experience of being embodied is the experience of of my being situated in the world. This is reflected in the linguistic fact that I have no use for the concept of a body that is not someone's body and which as such is contrasted with my body. The concept of an impersonal body is secondary and derivative – the concept of a body, contrasted with my body, but denied to be the body of

[1] *B.H.* p. 10.

anyone. A world of bodies uninhabited by anybody – that is by persons – would be a restricted world, abstracted from the actual world of personal experience. If the experience of existing is enjoyed by me, it is enjoyed in the company of other existents. Recognition of existence is a recognition of existing *with*: "to say: I exist, is to to say: I am in the world, I belong to a certain concert, I am involved in a certain consensus."[1]

The concept of existing, then, is complex in meaning. The difficulty this complexity presents to an economy in its exposition must be borne with patiently. It is important to avoid the danger, inherent in the wish for brevity, of presenting a mere caricature of Marcel's thinking upon the subject; for that thinking illuminates his conception of the person as much as it, in turn, is illuminated by the latter. If the concept of existing refers primarily to my situation as person, in one sense, under an aspect, it refers nonetheless to that situation as a whole. But this is to qualify the use of both 'aspect' and 'whole' in that context. And this, again, is to signal the metaproblematic nature of the question at issue. If existing be not, for Marcel, an aspect of my being in the world, in the sense of being a quality predicable of that being or a kind of specification of a fundamental act of being or a medium for being, there is still room for the question of whether I can have experience of myself as *being*, in a sense which is other them that of grasping myself as existing.[2] If there were hope of its being understood, use might be made here of the scholastic distinction operative in saying that existing refers to the situation '*totalis sed non totaliter.*' Another way of putting Marcel's position would be to say that while existing is no mere fact, neither is it an act. Here, again, with due allowance made for any distinction we shall later feel obliged to draw between 'existing' and 'being,' we might apply Marcel's observation that "however we may define *act*, it is evident that I cannot speak of the act of being – in the present case, existing – without being ready to give up the idea of conceiving anything resembling a subject of the act, a *someone* who fulfils the act."[3] Existing, then, cannot adequately be represented in any way divorcing it from the person who exists. And this is the reason for insisting upon the personal situation as the context within which an understanding of the concept of existing must be sought. Marcel's reflections on the subject have consistently moved towards the recognition of this fact since his break with Idealism. It has become a commonplace to remark the

[1] *P.I.* p. 154; c.f. *J.M.* pp. 169, 147.
[2] *M.E.* II. p. 32.
[3] *Ibid.*

difference in his manner of conceiving existence before and after the moment marking the interval between the first and second parts of his *Journal Métaphysique*. The difference is evident in the sharp distinction drawn between existence and objectivity in the second part in contrast with their equation in the first. A more significant development, however, is acknowledged by Marcel himself in a note of January 1959, commenting on the radical change in perspective commanding his reflections from the latter half of 1943 and published with them in *Présence et Mystère*.[1] Whereas the earlier reflections stress "the obturating character of existence, considered in its density," the later focus attention much more upon "what precedes that density... which is upsurge or, in another manner of speaking, exclamation." Here, he draws a distinction between a philosophy of the existent and a philosophy of the existential. "The existent... is the slackened fire, already almost quenched. Whereas... the existential corresponds to the moment of discovery in which existence is attained or apprehended as the Thou." The distinction marks the completion of the transition from the idea of the opaqueness of the irreducible – and the existential is the personal situation at the very limits of its irreducibility – to the full recognition of its metaproblematic character.[2] It might be argued that the existential would, with greater accuracy, be termed 'hypoproblematic,' since it refers to the situation in its experiental immediacy and, through its 'submerged' participation in the world, in its 'transcendence' of the subject-object dichotomy issuing from problematic reflection. The distinction, however, loses its importance when we recall the fact that the reflection which discerns the 'hypoproblematic' character of the existential is itself metaproblematic in the full sense. The existential irreducibility of the personal situation is apparent only to a reflection which, recollecting that situation in its integrity, is simultaneously aware of its transcendent orientation. This means that the existential as such can only be inadequately described in terms of spatial or temporal metaphor. The existential is not a level that is left behind or a moment that is surpassed. To be aware of my personal situation as existential is certainly to be aware of that situation as pre-existing any awareness I can take of it; but it is also to be aware of its existentiality as a persisting and essential feature of my conscious appropriation of the situation in which I find myself. It is to be aware that my reality as person is radically existential in its structure; but it is likewise to be

---

[1] *P.I.* p. 146.
[2] C.f. *B.H.* pp. 11, 13; esp. p. 11, n. 1 and p. 13, n. 2.

aware of that existential structure as integrally involved in the conscious development of my potentialities as a person. To look at existing in this way is to adopt a quite contrary attitude to that adopted by the rationalist philosopher, be he empiricist or idealist, for whom the concept of existing may well appear either trivial or obscure. In place of obscurity, the density of existential experience appears to the meta-problematic philosopher as *clarté* – a brightness of intelligibility that may well appear as excessive, muddle not mystery, to the problematic eye that will only accommodate the meagre clarity of concepts it can successfully manipulate. To Marcel, there is always rather more than less to meet the eye in existing. One may prefer a philosophy of the computable, but *a priori* there is nothing in common experience to suggest that reality is such. The embarassment of the existential is that ambiguity of our condition which objective thought seeks compulsively to resolve. The existential, no more than the personal, is not computable: "Yes *and* no, that is the only possible answer where it is we ourselves who are in question."[1] The person, embodied, situate in the world, is an existential cross-roads. The existential, that is to say, exhibits the indissociable metaproblematic modes of irreducibility and transcendence. This transcendence is, to use phenomenological terms, horizontal and vertical – in Marcel's terms, participation and transcendence. But to see the existential as transcendent in its irreducibility is to be aware of it as emergent and this emergence as fulfilled in a conscious development of its existential exigencies: "the more we grasp experience in its proper complexity, in its active... and dialectical aspects, the better we shall understand how experience cannot fail to transform itself into reflection, and we shall even have to say that the more richly it is experienced, the more, also, is it reflection."[2] This will be true, however, only in the measure that reflection is open to the recognition of the existential character of our situation and this means abandoning the objective prejudice: "in the objective order there is no more place for revelation than there is for mystery: the two notions are complementary."[3]

Existential awareness, then, is itself an integral phase of personal awareness. To become aware of oneself existing is to become aware of existing personally and of this as the indissociable mode of one's existing. Not only are the essential conditions of either awareness

[1] *M.E.* I. p. 152.
[2] *M.E.* p. 97.
[3] *J.M.* 293; 'mystery' corresponds to the term 'metaproblematic'.

identical – recollection of one's integral situation as a being in the world – but their common interest is the identical situation of a being involved in the world of things who yet transcends that world and is aware of so doing. The question of whether and in what measure the concept of person exceeds in intension the concept of existing is, in Marcel's philosophy, the question of the relation of this latter concept with that of being. Whatever that be, it is clear that the existential is no mere stage surpassed in the person's progress towards ontological fulfilment, since it refers to a situation whose self-transcendence is an integral evolving. This feature of existing is thrown into relief by Marcel's emphasis on the existential as against the existent. The term 'existential' in its application to my situation as a whole stresses the fact of my involvement in my existing in a way that 'existent,' with its undertones of objectified subjectivity subjacent to objectively detachable attributes, does not.[1] Recognition of this feature of existing and of the existential character of our condition opens the way to a concrete philosophy of the person: "there cannot be... any concrete philosophy without a continually renewed and properly creative tension between the *I* and the depths of being in which and through which we are, or again without a rigorous a reflection as possible upon the most intensely lived experience."[2] Existential awareness introduces us to that experience of the transcendent, on whose possibility we heard Marcel insist, precisely through its recognition of the existential character of the personal situation as such. That is to say, the situation is no mere factual presupposition of whatever language we construct with which to talk about ourselves and the world in which we find ourselves involved prior to any thought we take or report we make of it. It is our condition. Its exigencies, therefore, must govern the development of our potentialities as persons, that is, as human beings. Those exigencies are not formally a *priori* in the sense of being discoverable independently of the awareness we take of our situation or in the sense of defining ourselves as existent in abstract isolation from our situation. They inform an awareness that is primitive in that it recovers the original sense of existing that is integral to the situation itself as its fundamental and omnipervasive orientation. "The characteristic of the existent is to be involved or inserted, that is to say, to be in situation. Wherefore to abstract it, while pretending to posit it, not merely from such and such a particular

---

[1] C.f. *M.E.* II. p. 23, where Marcel expressly rejects the notion of being as a property in any sense or as a "sort of nakedness of being which exists before qualities and properties and which is later to be clothed with them."
[2] *R.I.* p. 89.

situation, but from any situation whatever, is to substitute for it, if not a sheer fiction, at the very least an idea."[1]

The concept of existing, then, is *synidesic*, in the way we found the concept of person to be. This again straightway indicates a radical divergence between the existential point of view and either the traditionally empirical or the traditionally metaphysical – thereby intending the rationalist or idealist, for such indeed, it seems, is what many contemporary philosophers take the metaphysical to be. The world which the existential point of view opens up to us is not a totality of simple facts without necessary connection with each other; neither is the focus of existential inquiry a transcendental subject shorn of the concrete conditions of his existing. The concept of existing is no mere limiting concept; it enjoys positive meaning: "to think of existing is ultimately to think of the impossibility of any opposition here between being and appearance... the existential aspect is inextricably bound up with my own condition of being not only incarnate but also a wayfarer – *Homo Viator*."[2] The concept is negative only in its denial of the objective interpretation of existential experience which is itself negative – and necessarily so by reason of the strictly specifying function of its essentially characterizing process. To stress the existential as against the existent, then, is to point out not only the fallacy in attempting to conceive existing in divorce from the person who exists, but equally the fallacy in trying adequately to account for it while isolating the existent in his existing from the world in which he is thereby present and active. The exigency for transcendence, by which Marcel terms the urge to recover the existential import of our personal situation, is neither an exigency to get beyond experience, nor is it an exigency to withdraw within a subjectivity insulated from all contact with the world in which we exist. It is, rather, "an aspiration towards a purer and purer mode of experience," that is, towards an experience at once more "recollected" and for that reason more intensely "lived."[3] The experience remains, however, the experience of ourselves involved in varying degrees of intimacy with the co-inhabitants of our world and only as such is it the experience of the growing intimacy with ourselves. It is an experience that can be continually deepened precisely in the measure of its being an experience of myself *with* others: "I only constitute myself as interiority inasmuch as I become aware of the reality

---

[1] *P.I.* p. 113, 'idea' here refers to 'objective notions,' in Marcel's sense of the term.

[2] *M.E.* II. p. 27, 'incarnate' and 'wayfarer' refer to horizontal' and 'vertical' transcendence respectively.

[3] *M.E.* I. pp. 62–66.

of others."[1] The developing intensity of existential experience – and with it the differing though related "meanings" of existing – will thus become apparent only through a growing awareness of the increasing intimacy with our fellows to which we can open ourselves. This intimacy, in its turn, represents in its several degrees an ascending scale of conscious emergence within, and not from out of, our existential situation. "The genuine existential promotion," Marcel asserts, "is always an accession to an *us*, or to an *our*," immediately adding as rider, "on condition of this becoming for us a principle of intimacy and not of constraint."[2]

The introduction of intimacy into the consideration of existing indicates the peculiar significance of this latter concept in Marcel's philosophy that justifies the radical distinction he draws between existing personally and existing impersonally and his adoption of the former as a kind of paradigm case of existing.[3] Intimacy not only indicates the peculiar mode of experience that is existential and, in consequence, personal; it also indicates the peculiar mode of existing that is so experienced and, as such, is peculiarly personal. Marcel makes use of the term not only with regard to our experience of others as existing and of oneself as existing in concert with those others, but he uses the term also with regard to myself in relation to to my own existing. To stress intimacy as the mode of my own experience of myself as existing is to contrast such an experience with the mere acknowledgement of a fact. That is to say, the recognition of my own existing is not the recognition of myself as instance of any description however exhaustive. It is a recognition that is evoked in response to the central question upon which, so Marcel insists, all other questions hang. "It is the question I put when I ask myself who I am and, more deeply still, when I probe into my meaning in asking myself that question".[4] Quite obviously, then, this question is not one of identifying myself in any sense in which I might want to identify a total stranger who had wandered unbidden into my room. There are, indeed, situations where I might have to identify myself in this fashion to others. The identification then required would be in function of some specific and, therefore, quite limited interest prompting their question or of some definite rôle in which I serve their purposes. Conceivably, though more rarely, as instance the case of amnesia, I might have so to identify myself to

[1] *P.I.* p. 169.
[2] *P.I.* p. 160.
[3] C.f. *P.I.* p. 149, 160; *B.H.* p. 11.
[4] *M.E.* I. p. 98.

myself. In such a case, however, I should have become in effect a stranger to myself and part, at least, of my endeavour would be to establish for myself a place in the social scheme. In all such cases, the procedure for identification is precisely that which I should have to employ in identifying the errant stranger. Now, in every such case of self-identification, whatever the purpose behind it, there persists a common feature: I am trying to establish myself as 'somebody' and this I can do only in connection with and in opposition to other 'somebodies.' The identity recognized in my awareness of myself existing, on the other hand, – the identity answering to the question of who I am when, well enough aware of my public identity, I put that question – is not that of a 'somebody.' It is not the kind of identity established through objective description. It is an identity presupposed, indeed, by such objective description, if it is in fact to have any reference, but which still awaits recognition, however exhaustive that other process might have been. The utter irrelevancy of the kind of objective identity that establishes me as 'somebody' as an answer to the question of who I am – and with it the realisation of there being a real significance in raising this latter question – appears in the situation which Marcel cites by way of a kind of comic paradigm of all efforts to reduce the meaning of my existing to the more instantiation of predicates describing me, which has as counterpart the effort to reduce my ontological identity to that of a mystifying relation obtaining between the reified aspects of myself which objective thought discerns, be they termed states, experiences, or qualities. This situation is that in which I find myself when obliged to fill in an official form. "I have not a consciousness of being the person who is entered under the various headings thus: son of, born at, occupation, and so on."[1] That is to say existing is not acting a rôle, though it may involve me in acting many different rôles, either of my own or others' choosing. The same feeling of absurdity that invades me when forced to play the bureaucratic game of form-filling, allayed only by my consciousness of my ability to escape my official role by inventing another identity for myself, would recur were I forced to stick to that. It is certainly true that since I am myself and not somebody else, I must answer to the various identities corresponding to the different roles I play in life. It is equally true that there is within me an abiding sense of not being thus 'somebody': "from the moment when I start to reflect,

---

[1] *M.E.* I. p. 99; c.f. *H.P.* pp. 179–180, where the argument is extended to any functional identification of persons. Incidentally, Marcel's analysis points to an existential significance of the comic more profound than the social significance discerned by Bergson among others.

I am bound to appear to myself as a, as it were, non-somebody linked in a profoundly obscure fashion with a somebody about whom I am being questioned and about whom I am certainly not free to answer just what I like at the moment when I am being questioned."[1] Indeed, as Marcel justly observes in a comment upon Sartre's well-known portrayal of the waiter in *"L'Etre et le Néant,"* the very ability to maintain a rôle argues its effective transcendence and the establishment of a domain outside my condition of enacting it.[2] This fact, implicit in my recognition of the rôle as a rôle, indicates the positive character of my experience of being simultaneously "a somebody and not a somebody, a particular individual and not a particular individual." The experience consists in recognizing that "the definite characteristics that constitute the self insofar as I grasp it as a particular individual, a somebody, have a contingent character." This contingency can only appear as contrasting with a certain non-contingency of the self. The reality in relation to which the definite characteristic of my particular individuality appear as contingent cannot, therefore, be an object for me; for this would be to reduce it to one other among those specifications of itself with which it is contrasted. On the other hand, we must beware of jumping to the simple conclusion that "it is in relation to myself as subject that these definite characteristics of my particular individuality are felt to be, and acknowledged to be, contingent." The danger, against which previous discussion of the categories of having and being should have prepared us, is of treating myself, so conceived as subject, as in fact an object. While, as Marcel once again justly remarks, my relationship with myself is capable of indefinite specification, in the present context such specifications are seen to fall into two fundamental categories, corresponding with those of having and being: "I can treat myself as a stranger and, on the other hand, as somebody with whom I am intimate." It is this intimacy which is intended by saying that to experience myself as existing is to experience myself as subject in contrast with the definite characteristics which specify that existing.[3]

Now, this recognition of the essential intimacy of existential experience – of my experience of myself existing – has important consequences for our understanding of the relationship binding myself to my existing and, consequently, of that linking my existing self with the various aspects that could be specified within that existing, as also for our

[1] *Ibid.* pp. 99–101.
[2] *P.E.* p. 45.
[3] *M.E.* I. pp. 101–102. Here 'specify' is taken in Marcel's sense of the term previously defined.

understanding of the nature of my awareness of others existing. First, let us take the question of myself in relation to my own existing and approach it through the question of the relationship of my own existing self with the definite characteristics that constitute that self grasped as a particular individual. Recalling the findings of or earlier consideration of the contrasting categories of being and having, the answer is clear. My existing self cannot adequately be conceived, to employ phenomenological terms, as a mere series of unfolding profiles nor yet as something standing behind those masking profiles. There can be no question of a simple series: we must think of the existing self as present, manifesting itself, in each profile. Such an approach to an answer accords with Marcel's affirmation of the metaproblematic and with his parallel assertion that the objective is conceivable only on the basis of the inobjectifiable. The concept of a profile is secondary to that of the existing self of which it is thought to be the profile. Similarly, the concept of a series of profiles and, therefore, of its unity throughout its unfolding is secondary to and derived from that of the persisting identity of the existing self. Thus, the answer to the question of the relationship binding me to my own existing follows quite naturally: in any affirmation of myself as existing neither can the 'I' be conceived of as a subject apart from the 'existing' nor the 'existing' as a predicate apart from the 'I.' The existential affirmation must be taken as an indissoluble unity. There is a unity not only of the 'I' with the 'existing' but equally of the 'I exist' with its affirmation. The awareness of oneself existing is, then, as Marcel terms it, "an exclamatory awareness of self." "Existence and the exclamatory awareness of existence." he asserts, "cannot really be separated; the dissociation of the two can be carried out only at the cost of robbing the subject of our investigation of its proper nature; separated from that exclamatory awareness... existence tends to be reduced to its own corpse; and it lies outside the power of any philosophy whatsoever to resuscitate such a corpse."[1] The term, "exclamatory

---

[1] *M.E.* I. pp. 103–107; *J.M.* pp. 312–313; *P.I.* p. 162. This view of the existing self explains Marcel's rejection of the traditional term 'substance' – "for me the veritable substance consists in the object conceived as a relation between diverse predicates. Now the *this* of which I have spoken (the non-mediatisable immediate) is nothing of the kind." (*J.M.* p. 250). Scholastic philosophy, of course, donceives of substance in an entirely different manner. C.f. for example, F. C. Copelston, *Aquinas.* Pelican, 1955, pp. 80–85: "a substance is not an unthinkable and completely unchangeable x, entirely inaccessible to the human mind... what I experience is neither an unattached accident or set of accidents not an unmodified substance: I perceive a modified thing" (pp. 82–83). This point of view is clearly akin to Marcel's, c.f. also J. de Finance. "Etre et Subjectivité." Doctor Communis II. Maii-Aug. 1948, p. 245: "The idea of being... presupposes the apprehension of existence, I mean of *exercised* existence, for, without reference to it, *signified* existence would be only an empty conception... Existence in all strictness is not object of a concept."

awareness," expresses the pure immediacy of the existential affirmation. "That existence cannot be treated as a *demonstrandum* is something that we cannot fail to perceive as soon as we observe that existence is primary or it *is* not – that in no case can it be regarded as capable of being reduced or derived."[1] Since Marcel goes on to say that "here there is no question of referring," one would not be surprised to hear him express his willingness to admit that "the fundamental assurance we are dealing with here is of the order of sentiment or feeling." It would be rather silly, however, to dismiss the matter our of hand on this account without trying to find out what exactly he intends by this admission. He qualifies it thus: "provided it were explicitly understood that this *feeling* must not be intellectualised and converted into a jugdment, for any such conversion would not only change its nature but possibly even deprive it of all meaning." Here, it were well to recall that "intellectualisation" in this context means "objectively conceiving" and "judgment," the kind of proposition that "objective thought" deals in. Marcel is further concerned to distinguish "exclamatory awareness of oneself existing" from one's sense-experience. There is no question in his mind of substituting for the *Cogito* a "*sentio, ergo sum.*" "The *sum* itself, the affirmation, 'I exist,' seems to lie at another level (than that on which the process of inference can operate); above, as it were, and on the banks of every possible current of inference."[2] The verbal expression of this exclamatory awareness need not necessarily accompany it. If there be verbal expression of the exclamatory awareness, the awareness it expresses is neither antecedent nor consequent but simultaneous. The exclamation, moreover, is integral to its verbal expression, manifest through intonation, a feature of its meaning only inadequately conveyed by the typographical symbol of an exclamation mark.[3] One might be tempted to see in existential awareness a "poetic" experience and in its exclamative expression an "emotive," as opposed to a "referring," use of language. The latter distinction, as once current in a certain school of literary aesthetics, or even as used in the philosophic circles from which it derived, is foreign to Marcel: in his terms, it is a distinction that could only arise in a problematic context. Certainly, as far as Marcel is concerned, poetic awareness would be a development of existential awareness, conserving and fostering an insight that has its roots in the latter in a way objective reflection is incapable of doing; but, then,

[1] *J.M.* p. 154.
[2] *M.E.* I. p. 105.
[3] *M.E.* II. p. 39.

rather than explaining the latter, it would there find its own origin.[1] The exclamative utterance is neither non-sensible nor non-significant precisely because it embodies the existential awareness. There is no question of "referring," in the "objective" sense of that term, precisely because the awareness is immediate and non-inferential. It can, certainly, be said to be "emotional," but not in any sense excluding "intellectual," except in an "objective" sense of this latter term. At this level of experience – which in this degree of "purity" is of rare occurrence,[2] – there is no room for distinguishing the "emotional" from the "intellectual," because there is no play for distinction at all. Thus, we find Marcel asserting: "The distinction between the idea of existence and existence itself – an impasse in which philosophical reflection is always liable to get lost – must be rejected out of hand: I myself am unable to view this distinction as anything more than a fiction that derives its birth from the arbitrary act by which thought claims to transform into an affirmation of objectivity what is really immediate apprehension and participation."[3] This feature of existential experience in its turn explains an otherwise hardly intelligible assertion of Marcel's, that the affirmation, "I exist," tends to merge with an affirmation such as "the universe exists": "the universe itself also being the negation of 'something in particular' without thereby necessarily being reduced to the general and the abstract."[4]

The full implications of this "global character" of the existential affirmation, as Marcel dubs it, will presently become clearer. First, let us clear up the question of its "emotional" character. We have seen that the "feeling" in question is not to be objectified. This applies equally to the sense of my existing – "if the affirmation *I exist* can be retained, it is in its indecomposable unity, inasmuch as it translates in not only a free but in a none too faithful fashion, an initial datum that is not *I think*, not even *I live*, but *I experience*, and this word must be taken in its maximum indeterminacy."[1] As to the sense of my existing in the world –

[1] C.f. *H.P.* pp. 50–53. Commenting on the fact that the idea that designation consists in choosing a conventional sign destined to serve as substitute for what is designated, Marcel asserts that such a view, not entirely false, omits what is essential, insofar as this is non-functionalizable. "In every case (of functional designation) there is an elimination of this non-functionalizable residue that is, on the contrary, so mysteriously and certainly present where one is bestowing a name on a child just born. But what is remarkable is that our current thinking tends so much to move in the functional sphere that it has the greatest difficulty in measuring up to this kind of intimate core of designation. Yet it is clear that we are here at the common root of a certain magic and of all poetry." (pp. 52–53). C.f. *M.E.* II. p. 39.

[2] *M.E.* II. p. 39.
[3] *J.M.* pp. 314–315.
[4] *J.M.* p. 313.
[5] *R.I.* p. 26.

"does not a certain experience of myself as tied up with the universe underlie all affirmation of existence?"[1] One obvious reason, then, for acquiescing, with whatever reservation, in the assignment of existential awareness to "the order of sentiment or feeling" is the fact of thereby stressing the absence of any objective specification within that experience: "it is doubtless by an evocation of the pure act of feeling understood as an interior resonance that we will be best assisted, not to obtain an imaginative impression, but 'mentally to imitate' this presence that 'subtends' the 'integrality' of our experience and of any experience whatsoever."[2] Part of the difficulty both in grasping and in conveying what is at issue here lies in the uncertain state of the contemporary vocabulary of feeling and emotion.[3] Insofar as "emotion" applies to a total response to the situation awakening it – while "feeling" applies to a particular psychological function at the disposal of consciousness – or, consequently, to an activity (in the broadest, "non-objective," sense) not wholly under the control of the self (nor, therefore, to be subsumed under the category of "having") – while "feeling" is patient of manipulation by the controlling ego – "emotion" would be a more accurate term than "feeling" to apply to existential experience as such. On theother hand, the "exigential" nature of the experience, together with its holistic character, distinguish it from sheer "instinct."[3] Though we shall make free to use "feeling" in the present context, since Marcel draws definitively none of the distinctions we have adumbrated, it is important to take account of the emotional texture of existential experience – in the sense just given "emotional" – as well as to note the philosophic relevance of the emotional overtones of its exclamative utterance, which might well escape our notice where language is interpreted in terms of a too facile dichotomy into an "emotive" and a "referential" use. This emotional aspect of the experience must be appreciated, paradoxical though this seem to the objective mind, if the intellectual (as opposed to a merely rational) nature of the awareness it inaugurates is properly to be understood, Speaking of the mind that would understand experience in its original purity and living density – that is, of existential experience – Marcel asserts:

[1] *B.H.* p. 11; c.f. *P.I.* p. 143; "the bond uniting us with the world we live in is nuptial"; c.f. *P.I.* pp. 154, 162.

[2] *J.M.* 321.

[3] C.f. James Drever, *Dictionary of Psychology*. Penguin, 1952. Under 'emotion'; also James Hillman, *op. cit.* for an exhaustive account of the various meanings propounded together with a definition accommodating the several aspects of emotional experience they describe. (c.f. *op. cit.* pp. 246–289). Hillman's definition best accommodates Marcel's general view of emotion, allowing, of course, for the latter's hyperphenomenological context.

[4] C.f. Hillman, *op. cit.* p. 269, note 1 and p. 279, note 1.

Intelligence must become at once ardour and receptivity – both words together are required. If we place exclusive stress upon ardour, we cease to see how the mind can understand: intelligence seems no more than enthusiasm; but if, as is too often the case, dupes of (a) grossly material image, we insist on receptivity alone, we falsely persuade ourselves that understanding is receiving a certain content. Intelligence can in no case properly be compared with a content.[1]

Thus, while the exclamative awareness of self fulfils various functions severally attributed to emotion, it does so not in opposition to the workings of intelligence but as an aspect of intelligence, whether considered as awareness or behaviour, that is indissociably and inextricably bound up with it. And this is not surprising when we recall Marcel's understanding both of reflection and of the person: that the ultimately philosophic reflection is metaproblematic working with synidesic concepts and that the person, contemplated by such reflection and so conceived, is a totality transcending specification. That is to say that the existential moment, if we may so term it, is a moment that persists, while gaining in intensity and scope, throughout the whole evolution of conscious experience, as warp to its weft. Here we not only rejoin what was said of existing earlier in the present chapter but can understand more clearly the meaning of Marcel's approval of Hocking's assertion that "all positive feeling reaches its terminus in knowledge," that it "means to instate some experience which is essentially cognitive," that it is "idea-apart-from-its-object tending to become idea-in-presence-of-its-object," which Hocking terms "cognizance" or "experiential knowledge."[2] Taking "object" in its innocuous, phenomenological, acceptance as "that of which consciousness is conscious" and understanding "idea" dynamically as we have seen Marcel to do, it becomes clear that this "experiential knowledge," more intimate than any objectively conceived "acquaintaince with," is one in which "idea" and "object" fuse in the recognition of what Marcel would term "presence." This experiential knowledge is, then, simultaneously cognitive and affective: "Between love and knowledge there can be no real divorce. That divorce is only made absolute where intelligence is degraded and, if I may use the expression, cerebalized and, to be sure, where love is reduced to carnal appetite."[3] Rooted in an existential awareness that is indissociably cognitive and affective, consciousness

---

[1] *M.E.* II. pp. 65–66 (author's trans.). For a similar conclusion as to the non-essentiality of the production of a content to intellectual awareness from a contemporary Scholastic philosopher, c.f. Barry Miller, *The Range of Intellect.* Geoffrey Chapman, 1961, Chaps. 2, 4, and 9.

[2] C.f. William Hocking, *The Meaning of God in Human Experience.* Yale, 1922, pp. 87–88, quoted by Marcel, *M.E.* II. p. 92. C.f. *supra* pp. 53e54.

[3] *H.C.H.* p. 13.

grows into a full recognition of presence that is indissociably both knowledge and love: "the knowledge of an individual being is not separable from the act of love or charity whereby this creature is posited in what constitutes him as unique creature."[1] Thus, the noematic pattern of experience corresponds with the noetic: awareness of the person, myself or other, as existing develops through to full awareness of his being. That is, just as the ontological identity of the person – which is the subject of inquiry initiated by the question "who am I?" – lies this side and that of the objective identity established by problematic inquiry, so does the awareness recollected by metaproblematic inquiry precede and exceed, in its affective-cognitive unity, the dichotomy established by objective reflection between those twin, existentially indissociable features of personal consciousness. At the same time, just as existing involves, as integral constituent of the situation it inaugurates, the exigency for its own transcendence, so must existential awareness be regarded as initiating its evolution towards the full consciousness of love in which, precisely, that existential exigency is fulfilled. It is not surprising that the existential affirmation should be rarely manifest in the naked and original purity of the exclamatory awareness of existing or that common speech should lack distinctive forms to mark its expression.[2] Existing itself lies outside the narrow circle of particular interests to whose expression and communication the economy of everyday language is directed. Its affirmation, too, constantly eludes adequate symbolization: on the one hand, it is not itself one among those specific characteristics of which linguistic symbols are normally a function and, on the other, when symbolized it merges with the specified characteristics to form the symbolically expressed content of a yet symbolically unexpressed affirmation. Nor is this proposing "reality" as ultimate subject of every judgment; for Marcel, reality is neither sum, nor *bloc*, nor system:

To be able to speak legitimately of 'concrete approaches' there must be at least a presentiment or 'forefeeling' of something regarding which we can say: 'This is reality.' But such a way of expressing ourselves still remains unsatisfactory. For to say 'This is reality' is to *indicate* something; the designation can only bear on objects... Being cannot bei ndicated, it cannot be *shown*; it can only be alluded to, a little as some third person now disappeared is alluded to among friends who knew him formerly and keep his memory green. The comparison is acceptable only if the evocation does not convert the being who has disappeared into an object about which we are discursive and ratiocinative. The being in question, who has become active subject, must magnetize a certain silence charged with affectivity.[3]

[1] *H.V.* p. 129.
[2] *M.E.* II. p. 24.
[3] *J.M.* Preface to Eng. Ed. p. viii.

The existential affirmation does occur, however, and not only in moments of metaphysical wonder that something *is* rather than nothing, or of poetic insight into the unique value of some being encountered in its irreducible singularity, but also in those, perhaps, more tangible instances where love awakens or "where a being has made its appearance in the world, has burst into life – a birth, for example, or the completion of a work of art."[1] With respect to existing so *discovered*, "existence as we ordinarily conceive – or believe – it is in some way dross or residue."[2] One function, then, of the emotional element in existential awareness is to startle us into recognition of what escapes the notice of routine consciousness:

> There cannot be... apprehension of the real without a kind of shock. The mind accustomed to or, more precisely, installed in the humdrum routine of daily life either no longer feels it or else finds a way of blotting out its memory – whereas the metaphysical mind never quite resigns itself to that dull routine it deems a slumber. There is more than difference here: there is absolute contrast in the mode of evaluation.[3]

What compels our "salute or greeting" is not the mere fact of existence noted as such – the mental filing of a phenomenon into its appropriate and pre-established category or the opening of a fresh file for a category yet unrecorded – but an existence acknowledged as presence and in the acknowledging witnessed to be of value.

> We need to recognise clearly, (so Marcel concludes the *Metaphysical Journal*), the transition from existence to presence and I am wondering whether it is not through presence that we can effect the transition from existence to value. Is not that which has value also that which increases in us the feeling of presence (it is immaterial whether we are concerned with our presence or with the presence of the universe). In these reflection there is one essential point – they seem to make possible a transition from metaphysics to ethics; for our worth is decreased to the extent to which our affirmation of existence is limited, pale, and hesitant.[4]

Inherent in the existential affirmation, then, we find a recognition of value. To exist is to be of value. If this assertion is to throw any light upon either existing or value, the bond between them must be carefully disengaged. Noting that, if we consider the real use of words, stress is put upon "exist" only "in saying: such a thing or such a person exists or no longer exists – or in the case where existing signifies to be of value," Marcel observes that only in such cases is "existing equivalent to self-signalling."[5] Now, two facts about the bearing of existential affirmation

[1] *M.E.* II. p. 24; c.f. *H.P.* pp. 52–53.
[2] *P.I.* p. 167.
[3] *R.I.* pp. 88–89.
[4] *J.M.* p. 306.
[5] *P.I.* p. 167.

and, consequently about the meaning of existing itself emerge from this:
the affirmation bears upon the reality affirmed *as a whole* and it bears
primarily upon that being as *being* and not as *such a being* – that is, it
bears upon *ipseity* and not upon *taleity* which, precisely, was the contrast
made between the identity that is subject of the ontological question and
that established through objective identification. "The characteristic
of existence is to be originally *saluted*, but what is saluted is not existence,
it is the existent as *self-revealing*."[1] This statement merits some analysis.
To say that existence is saluted is to stress that awareness of existing
and the exclamative utterance that affirms it are simultaneously recognition and appreciation: "the exclamation in question is essentially
admirative."[2] But since the appreciation is equally recognition, the
existential evaluation is strictly commensurate with the existential
affirmation. That is to say that the value in question is as "global" as
the "presence" affirmed – a feature recognised by Marcel in his remarking that "value, more manifestly yet than presence is intersubjective."[3]
The value existentially affirmed transcends, therefore, any and every
particular evaluation operated by objective thought – precisely as
existing itself transcends any and all of the specifications in which
problematic inquiry issues. Here, in effect, is the existential basis for
the affirmation, central to Marcel's whole approach to the question of
the person, of the final convergence of Being, Truth, and Value. For,
if "the transcendence of Being is that of Truth with respect to those
methods and to those truths," respectively, deployed by and emerging
from problematic inquiry – "the limited truths to which science gives
access" and the methods of verification in reference to which such
truths are defined" – equally, "the principle of what we call value...
can only be *being*"; since "where values are allowed to be dissociated
from that central affirmation, with that they fragment and, at the same
time, are devitalized, reducing each to its own skeleton, to something
that is recognized to be only an idea – in other words, value no longer
adheres to reality."[4] As the concept of person is for Marcel the common
focus of ontological and moral inquiry and since, as we have found it to
be, the concept of existing is an integral and basic feature of the concept
of person, we may expect the convergence of Being, Truth and Value
to be manifest in the existential affirmation, its characteristic utterance,
and the situation from which it arises and from which it cannot really

[1] *P.I.* p. 165.
[2] *Ibid.*
[3] *P.I.* p. 157.
[4] *P.I.* p. 17; *H.P.* pp. 44–45; *H.C.H.* p. 129.

be separated: "at bottom, the method is always the same; it is plumbing the depths of a given fundamental metaphysical situation of which it is inadequate to say that 'it is mine,' since it consists essentially in *being me*."[1] Thus, if Marcel can affirm "the omnipresence of Being... the immanence of thought in Being... *eo ipso* the transcendence of Being over thought,"[2] without converting this into an assertion of a purely formal transcendental unity of the "I think" which since "it accompanies all my perceptions... might just as well accompany none,"[3] – "my thought demands being: it does not contain it analytically, it refers to it."[4] – it is because "all thinking goes on *inside* existence, is itself a mode of existence."[5] This is not to deny that, if thought be a mode of existing, it is one "which is privileged in being able to make abstraction from itself *qua* existence," but this abstraction, we have already seen, is "for strictly limited purposes."[6] The limited purposes are those of *thinking* in contrast with *thinking of*. While *thinking* "does not come to bear on anything but essences" – here, the strict equivalent of objectively specifiable meanings – *thinking of* restores the existential context in which all thinking – and all language insofar as it is a genuine *speaking of* – operates and this is a personal context: "Only a certain person can think *of* a certain being or a certain thing; This is very important." It is true, of course, that in thinking of persons or things we can abstract from their existing, in the sense Marcel gives that term, and by merely taking it for granted slide into the manner of mere thinking; but, on the other hand, "the more we fill in the context, the more we slide from just *thinking* to thinking *of*."[7] This filling in the context means precisely adverting to the existential situation in which my thinking develops and, if my thinking of those others who exist *with* me is really to be a *thinking of*, all the objective specifications my thinking makes of their reality must be consciously referred to that common ontological situation in which we co-exist: "the *us* without doubt reveals itself as much more profound than the *I*."[8] The *us* is revealed in the exclamatory affirmation of existing in a double transcendence, horizontal and vertical. The horizontal transcendence is manifest in "the *aim*, the intentionality" which, as Marcel says, "is at the heart of the exclamation" and "behaves

[1] *B.H.* p. 20.
[2] *B.H.* p. 36.
[3] C.f. P. F. Strawson, *op. cit.*, p. 103.
[4] *B.H.* p. 38.
[5] *B.H.* p. 27.
[6] *Ibid.*
[7] *B.H.* p. 31.
[8] *P.I.* p. 160.

as the affirmation of a *you also*."[1] We shall attend to this feature of existential awareness presently. What we would immediately advert to is that this appeal to recognition in the very heart of self-recognition is, with the latter, enveloped in an awareness of participation in being recognized as such only because it is recognized as co-participation. Thus, Marcel, speaking of the *"you also"* just mentioned, says: "This is what I have translated by the word co-participation; one could just as well speak of co-implication."[2] Awareness of existing involves awareness of co-existing and, with it, is involved in awareness of so co-existing with those others in a context wider than us: "we are involved in Being, and it is not in our power to leave it; more simply, *we are*, and our whole inquiry is just how to place ourselves in relation to plenary Reality."[3] If "Reality" and "Being" seem vague concepts, it is precisely because at the level of awareness which is that of existential affirmation in its exclamatory emergence "Being" appears not as the content of my affirmation but as an affirmation "of which I am the stage rather than the subject."[4] Furthermore, any attempt to specify its content takes place within that affirmation – as we saw when we recognised the impossibility of adequately symbolizing it – and which is, then, "an affirmation which I *am* rather than affirmation which I *utter*: by uttering it I break it, I divide it, I am on the point of betraying it."[5] And this is the meaning of participation. Recognizing that all my thinking and all my talking takes place within my existential situation, which itself at its point of emergence manifests itself within the affirmation of Being that transcends it, while present within it as unspecified term of the exigency that founds it, "I am led to recognize a form of participation which has the reality of a subject" and which "can not be, by definition, an *object* of thought."[6] Now, obviously, if I participate in Being, I am not Being; while the fact that such participation is manifest as co-participation equally testifies to its "given-ness," its priority, conceptual and ontological, not only with respect to any object specified by my thought or language but also with respect to any subject I recognize as transcending

[1] *P.I.* p. 162.
[2] *Ibid.*
[3] *B.H.* p. 35.
[4] *P.E.* p. 8.
[5] *Ibid.* c.f. F. C. Copleston, *Contemporary Philosophy*. Burnes Oates, 1956, p. 74: "The primary datum is not... either subject or object but the self as existing in an undefined and unarticulated situation. Man finds himself 'there,' within the area of Being. The consciousness of the self as a reflectively apprehended centre and of definite external objects, a consciousness which grows with experience, presupposes a pre-reflective awareness of existing in encompassing Being."
[6] *Ibid.*

the specifications I make of them. Atomism – "piecemeal realism" – Nominalism and Idealism – into which, Marcel justly observes, the latter easily slides – go by the board.[1] Equally, to speak of a participation is to speak of a reality which with respect to Being, understood as the full realisation of "the exigencies of which the word being is in some sense the bearer,"[2] is itself a diminished realisation of those exigencies which, nonetheless, since it is an active participation – as witness its exigency – it can increasingly approximate. If we speak, then, of the possibility of verifying such an affirmation, it cannot be in any sense of objective verification. Insofar as affirmation of existing is an affirmation of an existing towards being – whether considered as intentionality or exigency – its "verification" is fulfilment – "being is expectation fulfilled, the experience of being is its fulfilment"[3] – but fulfilment not of this or that specific function or this or that particular want, wish or need: the fulfilment can only be that of my being as a whole. What this might be will later command our attention. Enough to note here that such a conception of fulfilment equates Value with Being. Insofar as affirmation of existing is affirmation of participation in Being, no verification is required; for "to assert the metaproblematical is to assert it as indubitably real, as something of which I cannot doubt without falling into contradiction"[4] and this because the metaproblamatic – which, quite simply, has now come to mean Being with my existing and the co-existing that together are manifest in the existential exclamation as participation in Being – is, as transcendent, experienced in my existing as its comprehensive exigency and, as irreducible, experienced therein as the context of my existing and all existing. It is experienced, moreover, in the development of my existential situation into conscious presence as the fulfilment of the existential exigencies of that situation.

The contradiction, then, is not a logical contradiction between propositions. For the proposition that would try to express the meta-problematic affirmation would be of a quite different order from that denying it. The latter would take its stand in the problematic sphere where existing is either ignored or taken for granted; whereas the former is constantly referred to subjects as co-existing and in that co-existing to Being in which *we* participate. "'But if you are *certain* isn't it that you are shutting your eyes to doubt?' They are shut."[5]

[1] *B.H.* p. 35, 29, 107.
[2] *M.E.* II. p. 30.
[3] *M.E.* II. p. 46.
[4] *P.E.* p. 11.
[5] L. Wittgenstein, *Philosophical Investigations*. Blackwell, 2nd Ed. 1958, II. xi. 2   24 c.

Wittgenstein's laconic remark is echoed by Marcel's "An indubitable concrete must have assimilated doubt without expressing it."[1]; the former's observation, "The kind of certainty is the kind of language-game,"[2] by the latter's "Objective certitude tends to be depersonalized: it is certain that. Reference to a structure of which I can say indifferently that it is that of things or that of ideas. The case of existential certitude is quite different. There is no question of evacuating the subject, but of transmuting him."[3] Hence the rôle of emotion in "existential assurance," as Marcel calls it in contrast with the particular certitudes of objective thought.[4] Not that "objective certitude" is devoid of emotion for all its non-emotive pretensions: we have already noted Marcel's diagnosis of the "passion" informing the objective and the attempt to universalize abstractive method.[5] The existential emotion impels recognition of existential reality, while making possible that recognition through its disruption of the conventional set of which the problematic attitude is the expression and making possible the development of genuinely metaproblematic reflection by securing the attitude appropriate to it.[6] Existential emotion differs from particular – and, therefore, "problematic" feeling – in important respects: it is "total" and it is indissociable from the intellectual recognition of which it is an essential, integral, and persistent feature. It is not a mere feeling of being "such and such a particular, existing, empirical ego," but a felt participation in being, recognized as such. It is, as feeling, the fundamental feeling of being in situation, of co-existing with others in being. Its indubitability arises from the fact that here doubt – which occurs where my existing is called in question by someone else or by myself treating myself as someone else – finds no gap in which to insert itself.[7] "We are in a sphere where it is no longer possible to dissociate the idea itself from the certainty or the degree of certainty which pertains to it; because this idea *is* certainty, it *is* the assurance of itself; it is, in this sense, something other and something more than an idea."[8] Hence, there can be no question of passing verdict on a proposition: it is a matter of "recollecting" oneself within one's experience and one's experiencing with oneself.[9] As J. L

---

[1] *P.I.* p. 92.

[2] Wittgenstein, *op. et loc. cit.*

[3] *P.I.* p. 119.

[4] C.f. *U.A. passim.*

[5] C.f. *supra*, Chap. I; c.f. Hillman, *op. cit.* Chap. I and pp. 264–266, 285.

[6] For these severally recognized functions of emotion, c.f. Hillman, *op. cit.*; c.f. *J.M.* pp. 171–172.

[7] *J.M.* p. 311.

[8] *P.E.* p. 12.

[9] If Marcel here seems to imply that recollection involves detachment from experience,

Austin remarks in a context similar in the immediacy of the awareness it refers to: "How absurd it is really to say I am *giving a verdict* when I say what is going on under my own nose!"[1] We have, then, in the affirmation of Being – precisely as an affirmation existentially involved in the affirmation of my own existing – a touchstone of ontological value with respect to any particular affirmation I may make about myself or others. Any such affirmation will be of ontological value and significance insofar as it is a fulfilment of the fundamental exigency that founds me as a being. Thus, a feeling, for instance, will be ontologically significant in the precise measure that it is involved within my conscious assumption of that fundamental exigency; correlatively, of course, no feeling is of value whose intention is opposed to the fulfilment of that exigency.

Now, this is indeed to make personal existing the paradigm case of existing. Only a conscious being is capable of becoming aware of the ontological potentiality of his existing and so of the conscious assumption and deliberate fulfilment of the exigency that manifests it. Correspondingly, only a person is capable of the self-revelation that manifests such a potentiality in speech or action. Only such a being can say of himself or have it said of him: "I aspire to participate in this being, in this reality"; for only in him can this aspiration arise which is "perhaps... already a degree of participation, however rudimentary." The existence of things can only be manifest by resistance to my efforts to master them. No revelation of inwardness is possible in their case. Indeed, their whole definition will be in terms of the interest they present to me, my attitude to them can never be more than a function of myself – except in one respect: insofar, namely, as I am aware of not having given them their being. But even this awareness is always a function of the awareness of my own existing as participation in Being. With things, I can never make the transition that I can make in the case of persons which, though it remains within the consciousness of our common participation in Being, is, nonetheless, a transition to beings. The manifestatory nature of existing – the "self-signalling" noted earlier – is "an appeal to the act of discrimination"; but the discrimination must be consonant with the demands of the existential situation which manifests personal existing as a special mode of participation in Being.[2] That is to say that

---

it is clear from the context and from later reflections on the subject in the Gifford, Lectures that the experience from which I detach myself is objectified experience, experience as interpreted by first reflection. C.f. *M.E.* I. Chaps. III, IV, V. The passage just quoted from *P.E* points to a like conclusion.

[1] J. L. Austin, *Sense and Sensibilia*. Oxford, 1962, p. 141.
[2] *P.I.* p. 147.

in making transition to beings I become aware of centres not merely of functional interest but of a non-functional, loving interest, and this is in virtue of their being centres of conscious participation, responsible and responsive. As such, they are capable of a like awareness and appropriation of our common ontological participation and, thus, of entering into a conscious communion in which our common exigency for Being can find increasing fulfilment.[1] "Beings as such, *qua* interiorities, can only be to be recognized and loved; for as masters to be obeyed or as instruments to be deployed, they are not, strictly speaking, beings."[2]

This opens up a whole new vista of awareness of persons as such, whose modalities we must examine in our next chapter. Suffice it to note here that this awareness of persons as persons – in their full ontological significance – obtains only in loving or, at least, in those modes of being present – fidelity belief, hope – which, as we shall see, are love's preliminaries and can only be properly maintained within loving. This is not to deny that we can continually treat persons in a non-personal manner – and for the most part to our satisfaction – for the greater portion of daily life. But this is merely to recognize the extent to which that life is functionalized, organized in view of radically quite selfish interests, and that in the world it secretes about itself persons count as such for little.[3] To treat persons in this impersonal manner is to ignore what precisely is their deepest reality and to reject the attitude whith which alone it is possible to arrive at an understanding of their ontological significance:

The other, in so far as he is other, only exists for me in so far as I am open to him, in so far as he is a Thou. But I am open to him in so far as I cease to form a circle with myself, inside which I somehow place the other, or rather his idea; for nside this circle the other becomes the idea of the other, and the idea of the other is no longer the other *qua* other, but the other *qua* related to me; and in this condition he is uprooted and taken to bits, or at least in process of being taken to bits.[4]

Moreover, this is equally true of my own efforts to understand myself, not merely psychologically but philosophically. The possibility of misunderstanding is bound up with the very conditions of my existing which is that of a person and not of a thing:

I don't always communicate with myself. To demand that this communication should be there all the time, is to seek to confer on it a mode of existing which is that of the

[1] C.f. *P.I.* p. 178; *M.E.* II. pp. 60–61; *P.E.* pp. 9–10. *U.A. passim.*
[2] *P.I.* p. 169.
[3] C.f. *H.P.*, *H.C.H.*, *D.W. passim.*
[4] *B.H.* p. 107.

most rudimentary object, the nearest there is to non-existence.[1] Self-presence is not an invariant... I am not always invariably present to myself; on the contrary, I am more often alienated or decentred.[2]

It is just as important to note that this self-presence and the effective recognition of my own ontological significance develops always *pari passu* with my recognition of others: "Contrary to those who would invoke analogical reasoning to account for belief in the existence of others, it must be said that I only constitute myself as interiority inasmuch as I take cognizance of the reality of those others."[3] To add that the awareness of persons as such, present in loving and in the cognate or dependent modes of being present mentioned above, partakes of the indibitality of existential assurance would only be to invoke the principle of ontological evaluation we found to be implicit in any genuine recog- of existing.[4] If this mean that there are situations in which epistemological anxieties, queries, and methods are irrelevant, this but accords with common-sense and an understanding of what a personal situation really is. It were ludicrous, for instance, seriously to question the existence of someone I love: I could only envisage the possibility of such a question by abstracting myself from the situation in which I found myself and by somehow suspending my loving. There is, indeed, a question that can arise and which will have to be taken seriously. It is the question posed by death. For Marcel, my existing, as distinct from my being, involves the certainty of my one day existing no longer.[5] The question is whether I shall then cease to *be*. But the anwer to even this question cannot adequately be approached without taking into account the death of other persons or, since to be persons *in the full sense* for me they must be loved by me, without taking account of the glimpse of an answer that my love for them affords.[7]

With persons, then, existing ceases to be a mere fact of being-there, even the mere fact of being alongside others, to become a being *with* others in the full sense of the phrase. And to mark this distinctive character of personal existing, we can only use a term which is commonly used only of persons and with decided overtones of conscious participation: presence. "Presence signifies more and something other than being-there; in all strictness, it cannot be said of an object that it is

[1] *P.I.* p. 160.
[2] *Ibid.*
[3] *P.I.* p. 169, c.f. Strawson, *op. cit.* p. 102, although the latter's concern is with the person as point of reference.
[4] C.f. close of last paragraph but one.
[5] *P.I.* pp. 147, 167, 170.
[6] C.f. *P.I.*, pp. 181–193.

present."[1] Awareness of persons existing can only develop, if it is to remain faithful to the exigencies of personal existing, into increasing awareness of presence, in which, correlatively, presence itself is intensified. Now, to invoke presence is simultaneously to evoke the possibility of its manifestation or withdrawal, and, correlatively, of its acknowledgment or denial. The recognition of these possibilities as inherent in the very nature of presence darries with it the further recognition of the essential freedom of the person with regard to presence, his own or others', not merely in its acknowledgement but equally in contributing to its fostering and the fulfilment of the exigencies to which it bears witness. Thus, freedom has a double aspect, intellectual and moral. It is called into play by the encounter of obstacles to the recognition of presence and the experience of certain ordeals which, seeming to make nonsense of the whole idea of presence, tempt us to deny it any value and to withdraw our recognition. It is not so much a question, then, of verifying presence as of proving our attestation of presence in the face of those obstacles and of those ordeals. The nature of the ordeal that proves our attestation of presence will occupy us when we come to consider the various fundamental themes of invocation in which presence is attested – belief, hope, love, fidelity, whose nature appears most vividly in contrast with the respective negative responses to the ordeals that call them into play. The intellectual obstacles to recognition of presence arise from the ambiguity that our existential situation presents to a thought which has not yet affirmed or understood the possibility of affirming the metaproblematic. Ensconced in a problematic world, it is always possible to deny the possibility of the metaproblematic dimension of experience and thus make appeal to experience in support of that denial. With this aspect of the recognition of presence, we have already dealt at some length. There is, however, another aspect of our existential situation whose ambiguity presents a temptation to resolve it by a purely problematic interpretation. This is embodiment or – as Marcel terms the embodiment of persons – incarnation. Although we have touched upon this subject in connection with the contrasting categories of being and having, it merits some brief consideration here. We shall consider the kind of obstacle the fact of our embodiment might seem to present to a recognition of presence and how, within the terms of Marcel's philosophy, that obstacle is overcome. Our task is greatly simplified because the principles of solving the problem and of understanding embodiment as a feature of personal

[1] *H.V.* p. 18.

existing have already been disengaged within or examination of the nature of metaproblematic inquiry and of the existential affirmation.

Existence, awareness of self existing, awareness of self incarnate cannot, Marcel insists, really be separated.[1] If exclamatory awareness of oneself existing represents the point of one's conscious emergence in the world, "a certain presence of my body to myself" furnishes my existing with a consistency which, without it, it would lack.[2] My body appears as the centre of my communication with the world. Now, if it is indeed an object interposed, therefore, between me and the world with which I communicate, it is difficult to see how we can speak of my presence in the world: "to say that something exists is not only to say that it belongs to the same system as my body (rationally definable relations), it is also to say that it is in some way united to me as my body is."[3] That my body in relation to me, my body precisely *as mine*, cannot be defined as an object I possess and that, the relationship must be one of participation – exactly in the sense relevant to my participation in my existing – follows from our analysis of existing and was already made clear in the course of our discussion of having. Our present purpose is to see what light this throws on the relationship between our body and the world and, therefore, between the embodied person and the world in which he is situated. Now, it is precisely considered as an instrument that my body appears as something interposed between me and the world so that my communication with that world becomes a communication at secondhand. "I cannot avoid being tempted to think of my body as a kind of instrument, or, more generally speaking, as the apparatus which permits me to act upon, and even to intrude myself into the world."[4] This instrumentality can be considered under two aspects. To the objective mind, the person appears as acting upon and as acted upon by the world through the instrumentality of his body. In neither case, Marcel asserts, is the notion of instrumentality an adequate concept to employ.

First, let us consider the body as instrument of my action in the world. Here we must ask what being an instrument means and what are the limits within which instrumental action is feasible. Every instrument is an artificial means of extending, developing, or reinforcing a pre-existing power with which must be endowed any person wishing to make use of the instrument. In such a context, each of my body's

[1] *B.H.* p. 10; c.f. *M.E.* I. Chap. V.
[2] *R.I.* p. 27.
[3] *B.H.* p. 11.
[4] *M.E.* I. p. 115.

powers is a specific expression of its unity and, viewed objectively, my body appears dynamically and functionally as the *ensemble* of its powers, its unity that of an apparatus adapted to manifold purposes. Such a concept of the body is possible, however, only the father be view it in detachment, that is, contrarily to my fundamental experience of my body as *my* body. Furthermore, reducing my body to an instrument, I involve myself in an endless regress of body upon body: merely as an instrument, my body can only be the extension of another and non-instrumental body. "This body, which by a fiction modelled upon the instruments that extend its powers of action we can think of as itself an instrument is, nevertheless, insofar as it is *my* body, not an instrument at all." Instrumentality, in fact, is conceivable only on the basis of the non-instrumentality of the body that utilizes it.[1] As a corollary, the performance of physical actions ceases to present a problem. Such actions become problematical precisely in the way my embodiment becomes so: by being detached as a particular content from the context that unites them with me in one existing person. Take the question of raising my arm. "What I call the idea of raising my arm is only the abstract schematisation of a particular posture that I cannot really think of, or represent to myself, but only adopt, i.e. mentally reproduce." It is the embodied person who raises his arm, not merely his body in detachment from himself, nor one of his "powers." So viewed, the actual raising of my arm – or any other physical action I perform – ceases to be a problem: I raise it. No physical science, then, is possible, or necessary, regarding the transition from the idea to the act or of "what – by a vicious transposition – we think we can represent to ourselves as a communication between spheres that are distinct." My body is not an instrument of action: it is the way in which I am physically present in the world, though as we shall see this does not mean that my presence is purely physical. "Speaking of my body is, in a certain sense, a way of speaking of myself: it places me at a point where I have not yet reached the instrumental relationship or have passed beyond it." It is truer, then, to say that I *am* my body, but only in the negative sense of denying any cleavage between myself and my body that objective thinking introduces, contrary to the testimony of existential experience. The assertion, if it remain faithful to the existential experience in which it is grounded, cannot be taken to mean that I am nothing more.[2]

The other sense in which my body might be thought to be an instru-

[1] *M.E.* I. pp. 115–116; *J.M.* pp. 238–239, 323.
[2] *J.M.* pp. 321, 328–329; *M.E.* I. pp. 116; *R.I.* pp. 29–30.

ment is that of registering sensations. This involves picturing sensations on the model of the transmission and reception of sensory signals. The analogy, Marcel asserts, will not hold. The concept of sensory signal necessarily involves that of its decoding, the substitution of one set of data for another set different in type. In sensing, however, there can be no primary datum that can be translated into the language of sensation. The physical event prior to sensation, which I am supposed to be translating, cannot be said to be in any way a datum of mine. If not, whatever the modifications it produce in my body objectively consider-ed, we must postulate an intermediary between the physical event and the sense-datum, in order to provide the two objective sets of data and the code in which the elements of each side of the transaction, equated with each other, are accessible to the mind that the notion of translation demands. In that case, we are faced with the difficulty of explaining how this intermediary – postulated in order that the physical event be regarded as given and, therefore, conceived as akin to sensation in every respect except that of being sensed – is possible. Either this unsensed sensation is itself a message, although unregistered by the recipient – when the original problem recurs – or we must treat it as primary and unanalysable, in which case it is not a message. The analogy modelling sensation upon the transmission and reception of sensory signals breaks down: it assumes the existence of an unsensed sensum, whose nature is of necessity unknowable. And since this unsensed sensum is, except for being unknown and unconscious, a sensation, the existence of a sensory message presupposes that of sensation, however heavily disguised, exactly as we have seen any instrument or apparatus to presuppose the prior and non-instrumental existence of my body.[1] Incidentally, Marcel here lays a finger on the essential weakness of any analogy likening the sensing subject to a camera, radio or television set, or mechanical brain: finally, it is something else – *someone* – who actually senses what they produce. "Signal," of course, is used of electrical or chemical stimulus and "response" of reaction to them: the terms, how-ever, in that use, are analogical, and it can be quite misleading to use them, in that sense, as a "re-analogy" not merely of what they originally derive their meaning from – "messages" – but of what is presupposed by that source-concept itself. The stimulus, the chain of stimuli, and their final pattern, while a necessary condition for sensation to occur are neither a sufficient condition for sensation nor sensation itself.[2] To the

---

[1] *J.M.* pp. 317–319r *M.E.* I. pp. 121–124; c.f. *R.I.* pp. 37–39.
[2] *J.M.* pp. 268–271; c.f. *M.E.* I. p. 123, where Marcel warns against confusing "the

objection, "I must be affected *by* something," the answer must be that with reference to myself *qua* sensing it lacks meaning: "it only has meaning in the measure in which I cease to experience the initial state so as, however confusedly, to think" – i.e. objectively – "so as to detach myself from it."[1]

A rather similar concept forces itself upon us in the case of memory. It could be argued that memory, in the sense of recalling an experience, implies the conservation of a sense-datum. Such a notion clearly pertains to the category of having. Within that context, memory becomes a matter of conserving objectively distinct elements; itself, an aggregate susceptible of dispersion. This spatial idea of loss and dissipation, however, implies something spiritual. "I say that a whole is dispersed. This means that it ceases to be a datum given as a whole to the psychological activity to which I make reference... to lose is essentially to forget. Mnemonic experience is really at the root of the rudimentary experience to which people claim to reduce it." Recollecting the experience of remembering, it is impossible to credit the notion that the remembering subject is a *répertoire* of juxtaposed and discrete mnemonic events or entities. "It is better to say that the experience is incorporated into our being and that, in consequence, it continues to live on in us." The past as past is *present* to me remembering: "the past as past can no more be dissociated from the past as present to consciousness than the object seen can be dissociated from the so-called real object." Remembering, like sensing, like acting, is a way of existing.[2]

Of the embodied person, then, we must say that he is in the world as participating in it. This means that his distinction from others is no more insularization than his co-participation is a coalescence. Sensation is not interposed between me and the world in the manner of an object, no more than memory is wedged between me and my past. Insofar as we speak of them as media of communication, they are media *through which* the world and the past are present to me, not media *from which* I have to infer them. But, then, we should be speaking of communion with rather than of communication: "the world exists for me in the measure that I have relations with it which are of the same type as my relations with my own body."[3] We can weave together the variou

---

pertubation communicated to our organism and the fact that this commotion is given to subject"; c.f. Leslie Paul, *Persons and Perception*. Faber, 1961, p. 192.

[1] *J.M.* p. 185. The objection to "being affected by" is in its "passive" – as opposed to a "receptive" – acceptance.

[2] *J.M.* pp. 149–150; 176–177.

[3] *J.M.* p. 261.

threads of reflection on existing, embodiment, and sensation to get an idea of how we must approach an understanding of our sensual communion with the world around us. At the core of experience, yet pervading it, is the existential; dynamic in its stasis; participating in Being and, as so participating, personal; at the same time, in its stasis embodied and, as embodied, participating through its sensing with the surrounding world. The exclamative awareness of existing is indissociably linked with the non-objective awareness of my body as mine which, as Marcel says, is "a non-mediatizible immediacy," "at least in some degree continually felt," as such "conditioning for me all my feelings,"[1] and which must be recognized to fuse with existential emotion and its assurance that suffuse exclamatory awareness. Participating in the irreducibility of existing, my body participates in its transcendental orientation, in appropriate manner, so that it can be truly said to be *"in sympathy with things."*[2] Just as the non-instrumentality of sensing bears witness to my body's participating my existing, so does it witness my bodily existing's "immersed participating" in the world"[3]: much as my existing witnesses to my immersed yet emergent participating in Being. Now, this means that my embodied self cannot be regarded as merely passive with respect to the world nor yet as simply active. It is receptive. It welcomes the world and this is the true meaning of its being responsive.[4] Just as recognition of non-mediatizible immediacy transcends the opposition of subject and object and that of personal existing transcends it, so does recognition of my body's rdceptivity involve that of a reality that at one end of the scale – sensation-lies below and the other – fully developed personal, inter-subjective consciousness – beyond the contrast of passivity and activity. Now, there cannot be receptivity without a certain pre-ordination and pre-affectation.[5] The pre-affectation argues the body's being pre-disposed for sensing – and through and beyond it for perception and the whole gamut of awareness – by its physical organisation in co-operation with its physical activation by the surrounding world – so that my body is through and through "feeling," in a sense prior to the "feeling" previously invoked, a feeling that is receptive: a welcoming of the world that is at once active in its passivity and passive in its activity. The precise nature, organization, and distribution of this physical inter-activity, it is not the business of

---

[1] *M.E.* I. p. 125; *J.M.* p. 252.
[2] *J.M.* p. 261.
[3] *M.E.* I. p. 130.ff.
[4] *M.E.* I. p. 134.ff.
[5] *Ibid.*

metaproblematic reflection to define. That is a job for scientific inquiry on the strict understanding, however, that its findings are entirely conditioned by the problematic attitude that quite properly governs the inquiry and that, therefore, to be referred to the person *qua* person must be re-interpreted in the light of metaproblematic reflection. In particular, we can understand why there can be no science regarding the transition from the physical activity that is a prelude to sensing to sensing itself. The pre-ordination bespeaks my "pre-existing" my existing as exclamatorily experienced and the participation of my embodiment in that existing. This explains how awareness develops cognitively and affectively in step and all along the line. It further explains why affirmation and assurance is prior to doubt and denial. That is why we take for granted that things are as they seem. Indeed, the concept of mistake is derivative and unintelligible apart from that of the assurance with which it is contrasted. So that a mistake appears as the confounding of an expectation – but always of a particular expectation whose assurance is grounded in the fundamental assurance of existing. When it occurs we rightly suspect that has something had disorganized the body's pre-affectation – just as this pre-affectivity explains both the need for mistakes in order to learn and their possibility since it is the pre-affectivity of a being "on the move." Equally, we can understand that mistakes can arise for emotive reasons: that is, through a unreflected attitude adopted either in opposition to the ontological exigency as it manifests itself at successive levels or in detachment from it. Such an emotive attitude is not, however, emotion either in the basic or in the full sense of that word. It could be said to differ either by excess – whence "passion" – or by lack – whence "sentiment," in the "sentimental" sense – of that emotional energy that derives from the central, pervasive, existential emotion.[1] The terms, "passion," "sentiment," properly belong to the universe of problematic discourse to whose maintenance as only credible universe they can in varying measure contribute. Certainly, if we consider bodily disorganization or disaffectivity a source of error, my body itself appears capable of becoming in some degree, not merely *in abstracto*, but *in concreto* an object. That is, disease and malhabit seem effectively to detach my body from myself, so that it becomes something to control, precisely in the degree in which it behaves as object. Even then, however, my body never completely becomes *a* body. It could only do so in death – which from the problematic point of view appears the great and final mistake, – but

[1] C.f. Hillman, *op. cit.* pp. 269, 275, 279–285; c.f. also *J.M.* pp. 171–172, 296–297, 319, 324

then my body at death ceases to be not only *my* body but *a* body – a corpse, a congerie of "bodies" that are bodies only in a sense far removed from that enjoyed by "body" in the context of its being *mine*.

Finally, we must constantly remember that once awareness is viewed within its proper context – the existential context in which it arises and develops – "impersonal thought, which is the only foundation for objects, cannot be constituted," as Marcel affirms, "otherwise than on the basis of personal consciousness."[1] The existential experience of being embodied invites the further recognition that though in a certain sense I *am* my body, this is true chiefly as denial of the proposition that I am not my body.[2] Psycho-physical parallelism, materialism, and ephiphe-nomenalism alike must be discarded.[3] Their rejection follows from the recognition of my bodily existing as immediately participating in my personal existing. Moreover, my acting cannot be reduced to mere physical behaviour nor my activity as a whole to what is strictly tied to such behaviour. The integrity dissolved by abstracting my physical acts from my existential acting self is restored once I act and this re-integration is manifest in metaproblematic recollection of the situation as experienced. The person *qua* person, this suggests, can only be *per accidens* object of problematic inquiry: *per se* the person *qua* person is subject only of metaproblematic inquiry, the rôle of whose reflection – "whether this be exercised on *feeling* or on *acting* – consists not in cutting to pieces and dismembering but, on the contrary, in re-establishing in all its continuity that living tissue which imprudent analysis tore asunder."[4] There is no obstacle, then, to our recognizing in the person a presence that overflows the purely physical, nor to recognizing that this presence may reveal itself through the physical reality that partici-pates in it: "presence is something which reveals itself immediately and quite unmistakably in a look, a smile, an intonation or a handclasp."[5] It may be objected that nonetheless, I may mistake for my friend whom I expect to meet a figure at the Waxworks. There are short answers to this objection that spring to mind. One is to point out that looking for one's friend at the Waxworks is not quite the same as assuring yourself of his existence. Another is to say that to approach him in this manner is precisely to approach him as you might any object without waiting

---

[1] *J.M.* p. 254.
[2] *J.M.* p. 253; *R.I.* pp. 30–32.
[3] *M.E.* I. pp. 108, 116–117.
[4] *J.M.* p. 324.
[5] *P.E.* pp. 25–26.

for those unmistakable and immediate manifestations of presence: the warm pressure of a hand, the smile that lights a living face, the words of friendly greeting which require no inference to establish presence since it is already there transforming them. Of course, in a society where people consistently hid their feelings, refrained from all conversation, behaved like robots, one might find oneself wondering on entering a railway compartment whether in fact the figures seated opposite were persons. There is justification enough, however for our normal confidence that family, friends, and even chance acquaintances really exist and are real persons. That one's friends can successfully mask their feelings on occasion or hide their thoughts does not argue that they can never convey them and in other and more subtle ways than speaking. Indeed, one of the more common experiences of loving is the difficulty people in love with each other find in keeping to themselves their thoughts, feelings, hopes, anxieties, when they have need to do so. The justification we spoke of is not exactly proof; but then proof in the context of personal awareness and with respect to what is personal in it is neither needed nor to be expected. Proof, in the sense of inductive or deductive inference, operates within a strictly problematic context. Metaproblematic reflection, which justifies the unreflected existential assurance that lies beneath the general unreflected assurance of common experience, is justification only by way of recognition. For that precise reason, because the reality on which it bears is metaproblematic I can, by remaining ensconced within the problematic, fail to recognize it and so pronounce the justification a nonsense.

Nothing that has been said can be used to deny the legitimacy of problematic inquiry that keeps within its proper scope. Thus, even in the case of objective identification, the procedure we found quite justified. There is no practical difficulty in identifying in this sense, nor should there be a theoretical, for there is nothing arbitrary in the procedure once we realise that it operates in virtue of a particular and, therefore, objectively definable interest. Nor need there be anything arbitrary in the selection of this interest. It is a practical problem, in principle practically soluble. What would be arbitrary would be to restrict significance to what is amenable to that kind of identification or to admit as meaningful only what satisfies inquiry operating with concepts so defined. That the person *qua* person is not appropriate subject for problematic inquiry nor the meaning of that concept definable in terms of the kind of descriptive identification it operates is the burden of Marcel's criticism of problematic method and of the spirit informing the attempt to universalize its value.[1] Neither, again, does this mean that nothing significant can be learnt about persons in general or in particular from such inquiry. What it does mean is that there is no justifiable transition from such information to a general theory of the person without shift of attitude and change of method to the metaproblematic; nor, in the case of a particular person, will there be from the problematic standpoint a hope of recognizing his value as person – a value which he only ever partially fulfils yet which, in the partial fulfilment, transfigures him entirely. At this stage of our inquiry the question of value gains increasing importance. To see the person as existing is to see in him an exigency for ontological fulfilment – "I am, present to myself as embodying certain values or at least as nourishing certain exigencies."[2] – and his body "as reserve of the future."[3] Value and presence, however, we have seen to be correlative and to develop in unison through communion with other persons: "the more my existence takes on the character of including others, the narrower the gap which separates it from being; the more, in other words, I am."[4] It is to the nature of this communion and the essential themes of our invocation of the presence of other persons, that our inquiry must now attend.

[1] C.f. H.V. p. 32
[2] *P.I.* p. 143.
[3] *P.I.* p. 111.
[4] *M.E.* II. p. 35; c.f. *P.,.* p. 160.

CHAPTER IV

THE FELLOWSHIP OF BEING

"Person – commitment – community – reality: here we have a chain
of notions, not strictly deducible from each other... but capable of being
grasped in their unity by an act of mind which is fittingly described not
by the sullied term of intuition but by the too little used one of *synidesis*,
the act by which an *ensemble* is maintained under the mind's regard."[1]
Already we have seen that, within the context of Marcel's philosophy,
the meaning of the concept of persons cannot adequately be understood
in abstraction from the existential situation that is his. Not that this
means that the concept can be understood only in explicit reference to
this or that particular situation in which at any given moment a person
finds himself. The situation in question is the fundamental situation of
existing bodily in the world, of which any particular situation is a
concrete specification in the sense of being an integral moment in the
total evolution of the former – insofar, that is, as it represents a further
degree of fulfilment of the ontological exigency that subtends, pervades,
and directs the latter. The recollection within which metaproblematic
reflection operates, and which is but another name for *synidesis* is therefore, a withdrawal from experience only in the sense of being a withdrawal in total concentration from the fragmented experience of the
world of problematic reflection or from the unreflected experience of
routine consciousness into the deeper, reflected experience of ontological
communion in which self and other are contemplated in the fellowship
of their common participation in Being.[2] For, metaproblematic reflection upon the existential situation of the person has shown it to be
a participating in Being that can be indefinitely intensified, subject
only to the limitations inherent in my mode of existing or which I may
find in the several particular situations through which it develops. At
the same time, this participating was shown to be essentially a co-
participating. This means that ontological fulfilment will be realised
strictly in the measure in which the intersubjectivity manifest in *co-*

[1] *H.V.* p. 27.
[2] C.f. *supra* pp. 51–52.

existing at the exclamatory level of awareness and in *consensus* at the embodied is in turn realised in *presence* at the fully reflected level of personal experience.

Presence, we found to translate more nearly than any other word the mode of existing that is personal.[1] And since the existent cannot be effectively detached from his existing, presence equally signifies the person existing, in this use effectively pointing the contrast of that existing with objectivity and with impersonal existing. Strictly speaking objects cannot be said to be present; while quite early, as Marcel observes, awareness of existing, which might conceivably be attributed to animals, develops into appeal for personal recognition by other persons that marks the transition from exclamatory awareness of existing to the conscious appropriation of the existential situation and of its exigencies.[2] Whatever "claim to recognition" an animal may be said to make, it never emerges into the *"toi aussi"* which we found to be at the heart of existential exclamation.[3] "Presence," then, like "existing" is primarily ascribable to persons and only in diminished sense to the impersonal. The impersonal assumes whatever it does of presence only as function of my own presence. Any reverence I show to impersonal beings, if it be not a matter of mere sentiment, is an extension of my recognition of my own participation in Being, tempered by the recognition of their inferior degree of so participating. Presence, in its essentially personal context then, can be seen to bear its distinctive marks of appeal, response, and fellowship in a degree that transcends not only the just-being-there of objects but also anything resembling these features that is discernible in impersonal existing. It must be remembered, moreover, that presence, no more than existing, is not an invariant – and this for the very reason that it is personal. Similarly, the concept of presence can be understood only with reference to experience that is in the full sense presential and not with reference to those debased experiences of which the term is used only in a diminished sense. These various aspects of the concept emerge in focus, if we attend to what being present really means in its concrete instance.[4] For one thing, we should not say of a person that he was really present at a meeting of which, in fact, through lack of interest and consequent attention he could give no adequate account, even though he should have happened to be there. Again, we cannot say of every encounter

[1] C.f. *supra* pp. 59, 76, 84–86, 92–93.
[2] *H.V.* p. 18.
[3] C.f. *supra* pp. 78–79, 82–83; c.f. *P.I.* p. 162.
[4] C.f. *M.E.* I. pp. 220–222; *R.I.* pp. 48–50.

between persons that it represents a communion of presence, unless and precisely to the degree in which the persons encounter each other as persons. Someone, for instance, can be there in the same room with me, audible, visible, tangible; yet I can sense well enough that he is not present – his presence does not make itself felt. It is not a matter of lack of physical communication, yet something essential is lacking. As Marcel remarks, "he understand what I say to him, but he does not understand *me*" – echoing here the colloquial idiom: "you're not *with* me." In fact, this "communication without communion, unreal communication," can have the odd effect of making my own words sound strange to me: "this stranger interposes himself between me and my own reality, he makes me in some sense also a stranger to myself; I am not really myself while I am with him." Conversely, it is common enough occurrence, except in society completely devoid of charm – as would be, significantly, a society in which those one encountered were regarded purely in function of one's particular interests – to meet people whose presence does really make itself felt and to experience in the encounter a spiritual refreshment, in the full sense, recreative: their presence "reveals me to myself, makes me more fully myself than I should be were I not exposed to its impact."[1]

Now, it is clear that the person who is centre of either appeal or response in such experience cannot be reduced to any specifiable content such as body or mind: it is the person entire who is recognised as present or who makes appeal for such recognition.[2] This, disposes, then, of any suggestion that by presence is meant a naked encounter of mind with mind. The concept of *a* mind has just that problematic use and is open to the same kind of criticism as that enjoyed by the concept of *a* body. On the other hand, the occurrence of the objective concept of mind points, as did that of the objective concept of a body to embodiment as an irreducible and inobjectifiable aspect of personal existing, to spirituality as an equally irreducible and inobjectifiable aspect. At the same time, the recognition of the non-instrumentally of the body in sensation and action, together with the acknowledgement of the participative character of each, removes the need of inference in such encounter: the need will only appear for a mind that adopts the problematic attitude. It is, nonetheless, undeniable, that the peculiarly spiritual aspect of presence is manifest more clearly in some people than in others. One such instance of its manifestation is apparent in the experience of "charm." Now, charm, wherever it is met with in its genuine

[1] *M.E.* I. pp. 222–223; c.f. *J.M.* p. 291.
[2] C.f. *H.V.* pp. 75–78.

form – and not as specious mask which deceives only because it is backed by some more tangible, downright physical, attraction or finds in the deceived an easy entry by way of some particular desire that moves them – charm appears a certain margin to personality: "It is the presence of a person spreading out beyond what he actually says and what he actually does... It is an over-plus, a beyond. Someone has charm if he easily sprawls out beyond his virtues, if these seem to spring from some distant, unknown source. And only the individual, in direct contact with another individual, can feel his charm."[1] We may add by way of rider to this account, perceptive though it be, something recognized elsewhere by Marcel in different terms. This is the fact of a person's finding another charming who does not normally appear so to others and this in no mere subjective sense: witness persons in love with each other.[2] The experience of charm gives the lie to those who scoff at any idea of there being necessary a certain mutual *rapport* between persons for them to experience each other *qua* persons. More importantly, it points to an understanding of moral value that places it beyond the sterile conflicts of "objective" with "subjective" theories. Charm and presence, of which charm is but a manifestation especial in its intensity, are a revelation not of value in the person but of the person as valuable and precisely as person. That is to say, this personal worth does not reside in any function that the person can perform. Neither is it any specific quality that can be objectively detached from his personality as a whole. It is that integral worth in which those particular values must participate, if they in turn are to persist in value. At the same time, it is clear that this integral value of being a person must, if it is not to remain an unrealised potential, be expressed in specific actions. Their evaluation, then, can indeed provide a clue to the extent to which my personal and ontological value is realised but only if approached within recollection, reflected upon metaproblematically, and referred to myself integrally *qua* person. This means, in fact, that any such evaluation remains necessarily incomplete, always in some degree open: the person *qua* person cannot function as content of our judgment.[3] This does not mean that a particular action can never be condemned nor a particular person found guilty of its perpetration and

---

[1] *M.E.* I. pp. 222–223; c.f. *J.M.* p. 291.

[2] There may be something mysterious, but certainly nothing mystical in this. It is an instance of what Marcel terms being "a connoisseur of reality." Its absence may be compared with Wittgenstein's "aspect-blindness" which he finds "akin to the lack of a 'musical ear'." C.f. *Philosophical Investigations.* II. xi. p. 214e.

[3] C.f. *J.M.* pp. 64–65, 216, 232–233; *H.V.* p. 197.

sentenced accordingly. Such condemnation, however, bears only on the crime considered as fact. Apart from the impossibility of assurance of the person's ultimate and inward guilt except by way of his own perceptive and free confession – which he is not always in a position to make nor yet to judge himself competent to make – presence testifies to an abiding and yet unrealised potential of value in him, the recognition of which forms the basis of our hope for, and of his claim to our co-operation in, his regeneration. There are two circumstances where hope might seem deprived of any such basis; death and physical or psychological impairment of the personality to the point of excluding further moral development. Of either case it may be said that despair of the person concerned derives from refusal to recognize in him anything that could survive such extinction or eclipse of existing; while the "moral state" of the person in question at the time of the catastrophe must remain a complete mystery for us insofar as he is now beyond response. Similarly, we are not precluded from advising on the moral value of a particular course of action in particular circumstances. Such advice, nonetheless, must be tempered by two considerations: the first, of what being a person means as such, for to that value as the value to be further realised in the action its project must be referred; the second, of the particular circumstances of the person involved in the project and that sympathetically in the full sense of this word, for that is the situation in which the personal value as such is to be incarnated. It might be objected against such a theory that moral value like presence – and in that context the morally valuable becomes quite simply *the* valuable to which any other value must be referred – that, just as we might find someone charming company despite, for instance, his subtle egoism or refined sensuality, so we can cherish and value what is not strictly speaking morally valuable. But this objection dissolves once it has been clearly stated. For, the theory we have just been considering involves a clear and just distinction between the valuable *simpliciter* and what is a value *secundum quid*, between what is cherished – in the final analysis – *propter se* and what is cherished *propter aliud*; which is but another way of marking the distinction between value metaproblematic and value problematic, the value one *is* and the values that can be *had*, the valuable and values.[1] In fact, it is only by ignoring, or by deliberately suspending recognition of, the valuable in the first sense that one can find a value in the second sense in what actually conflicts with the former.[2]

---

[1] C.f. *H.V.* pp. 202, 213; *H.P.* pp. 44–45.
[2] C.f. *H.V.* p. 200.

Finally, to speak in this way of the valuable is to see in it a moral beauty – ultimately, for reasons by now familiar, *the* beautiful[1] – a presence, that is, which suffuses and can quite transfigure the entire person, lending to his moral acts the freedom of sheer instinct. It is quite likely this feature of "the good man" that has led some thinkers to postulate a moral intuition or to see in "goodness" a non-natural, directly perceived quality. Morally speaking – which in the personal context is equally ontologically speaking –, however, value or beauty, no more than presence, cannot be abstracted from the person in the manner of an objective property or specific characteristic. The "good man," *simpliciter*, is he in whom the human ideal is fully incarnated. In those who most nearly approximate that ideal, whom met with in our concrete experience we call "saints," it shines out unmistakably. We must not forget, however, that the grace of their moral performance derives from the discipline of long practice and their direct discernment of the valuable in any situation from a connaturality with good formed by arduous experience.[2] For the ordinary man, moral discernment is the fruit of patient reflection and of action that effectively embodies it, of patient schooling of his will. His lack of the charm and grace of saintliness must be compensated by as clear sighted a vision of his distance from the ideal and of his propensity to its betrayal that accompanies human presence like a shadow. The fact that he is a person and so shares in all the exigency of the human condition makes it possible for him in certain cases to see immediately what is requisite for or conducive to that ideal's fulfilment: but he has to be on constant guard against the danger of misinterpreting the way in which that ideal can be embodied in particular circumstances through lack of sufficiently deep reflection or of the goodwill to undertake it. The concept of a human ideal that represents the ultimate pitch of presence and, consequently, the ultimate significance of being a person would seem to argue a recognition of something like the traditional concept of "essence." This question, however, is best left aside until we have completed our inquiry into the essential modes, in which, in the light of Marcel's concept of the person, presence develops in intensity and so approximates its ideal.

The concept of person that involves the concept of the person's presence in the world and, in and beyond that presence, of his presence

---

[1] Although he has never formally treated of the concept of beauty, Marcel has told the author that he would approach it in a Platonic manner.

[2] C.f. *M.E.* II. p. 140. On the significance of saints, c.f. *J.M.* pp. 5–6, 73, 82–83; *P.E.* p. 20; *B.H.* p. 174; *R.I.* pp. 190–191.

to himself and to other persons inhabiting his world involves a concept of personal activity that transcents the concept of purely physical behaviour as much as it transcends the concept of purely mental activity or of an dual activity that is both in parallel. If we consider the human act in the context of Marcel's concept of the person, it is clearly a moral act, an act of the whole person, a way of his being present that is, consequently, quite irreducible to any objectively specifiable element of the physical behaviour in which it is embodied or to the physical aspect of his behaviour as a whole. So viewed, certain essential features of the personal act emerge. Acting is opposed to mere velleity. To act is to commit myself and so to cross the threshold of the "yes and no." But this very committal argues the non-exhaustion of my act's significance by the apparent achievement of its mere *doing*. As committal, the act is by its nature responsible and unthinkable outside its personal reference. That is to say, it is the more act, the less I can repudiate it without at the same time repudiating myself. It is precisely this feature of his acting that distinguishes the person as such from the mere individual, type-instance, "anybody" – "*l'on a l'état parcellaire*" – who is essentially anonymous.[1] Clearly, then, the act as such cannot be considered in abstraction from the person in whose being it is incorporated by virtue of *his* acting without thereby losing its deepest significance and its ontological value. If we look at the act as essentially responsible and committed, we can see that in it the person assumes himself:

Act is something to assume; that is to say that the person in acting has to recognize himself in it; but it is only itself act by virtue of being that by which this further advance of the person is possible; it is, then, interposed between the person and himself. It is in the act that is realized the nexus through which the person is conjoined with himself; but it must be added that he is not outside this conjunction. A being not so conjoined with himself would be in the strict sense alienated – and therefore incapable of acting.[2]

In fact, the act can only be an interposition between the person and himself in so far as he dissociates himself from it, either by viewing it objectively or by repudiating it. His assumption of his act not only reintegrates him in his acting and, by the same stroke, his acting within his own existing, but it also reintegrates his whole life within his living present. It is recollection lived. That the personal act is an active integration and assumption of the person's existential situation is fairly obvious. In acting responsibly and with committment, I confront my situation. This confrontation involves its prior appreciation – not

[1] *R.I.* pp. 139–145.
[2] *R.I.* pp. 149–151.

merely in the sense of reckoning up my chances and the possibilities opening up before me, but in the deeper sense of evaluating the situation with reference, therefore, to the fundamental orientation of my being. "For confronting is exposing myself, that is, orientating myself in a certain determined direction; and only appreciation allows me to fix this direction."[1] That this appreciation involves an orientation towards the fulfilment of my fundamental ontological exigency follows from what has earlier been said of personal value. Of course, not every act I perform will have this conscious orientation. The more mechanical my acts, the less personal they are, the less acts in the prime sense of the word. But even such acts participate in my personal value in the measure that they are mine and in the measure that they are incorporated into my more conscious, moral, and truly personal activity as conditioning its fulfilment. At the same time, while confronting my present, I also confront my past and my future. This requires a little reflection. I confront my past much in the way that confronting a situation in shich I find myself, I assume its responsibility as I do the responsibility of my act and treat as my own.[2] But to do this is to confront my past not as an object but as my life in so far as it has been lived. Now, my life insofar as it has been lived is not something that can be reproduced adequately in any narrative of its events; it becomes alive only by being relived in memory and so incorporated with in my living present. Neither can my life be identified with the works I have produced: so produced they persist in their own right, open to appropriation by anyone who, interpreting them for himself, makes them in some sense his own. No judge, moreover, can sift out from among the various possible interpretations what is most truly expressive of myself. Interpreting the work myself, I reappropriate it by incorporating it into my living present. Similarly, the acts I have committed, as committed, lie outside my present grasp, save insofar as they have contributed to the creation of the person I am and in the measure that, consciously assumed by me in their enacting or in the accepting their responsibility, they become integral to my present self. My life as already lived, then, is neither an inalterable deposit nor a finished whole.[3] It is not a finished whole, for, as incorporated into my present – the only sense in which my life is still *my* life –, my acts open out into my future. Equally, my life is not inalterable, since, even as already lived, it is *my* life, its value therefore integrally

[1] *R.I.* p. 149.
[2] *R.I.* p. 151.
[3] C.f. *M.E.* I. Chap. VIII.

involved with the value that I am – a value in its turn only in part realised, still in part realisable. In this light we can understand the ontological – and, therefore, the ultimately moral – significance of self-criticism and regret. Certainly, by acknowledging that I have acted wrongly, in the moral sense, I do not thereby undo the material harm resulting from my action. Certainly, too, any regret I express requires, if it be genuine, sincere effort to mitigate the harmful consequences of my fault. But acknowledgement of and regret for my misdoing, besides being requisite conditions for such concrete efforts of reparation, are prelude to that re-orientation of my life with respect to the future, without which criticism and regret would remain sterile, empty gestures and through which my past life once more participates in the value that I am – the value which as person I have realised and of which I am still the promise. For, in judging my past life deficient in its value, I judge it with implicit reference to what in a certain sense I am and what my life manifestly is not. I am larger than my life and my judgment of it, that makes sense only if I do not strictly coincide with it, is possible because my presence *qua* person testifies to this non-coincidence.[1] Finally, then, in the personal act, I not only reintegrate my life as lived with my life as I am living it, but my life as I am still living it with my life as yet to be lived. Insofar as I am still living it, my life appears to me as something to be dedicated. In my concrete experience of living, the vivid awareness of being alive is fluctuating. It is a function of the meaning I can give my life. The more my life is geared to the fulfilment of some purpose – and the more important that purpose can appear to me – the greater my sense of being alive. Conversely, tedium is a function of the lack of interest in forming my life, to the extent that total lack of it issues a total tedium akin to, if indeed not identical with, despair.[2] Clearly, however, no particular interest is proof against the destructive irony of objective criticism. The only purpose that can withstand such criticism is the fulfilment of that fundamental exigency which we found to be the dynamic correlative of personal value – the person as valuable – *simpliciter*. In the consecration of my life to the fulfilment of that overriding purpose, the less it becomes a series of acts and the more it takes on the figure of an unique act.[3] This explains why self-sacrifice – for a person, for a cause – can appear to the person sacrificing *himself* with his life – indeed in any sense at all – not as self-

---

[1] *P.E.* pp. 12–13; c.f. *M.E.* I. pp. 176–177; *B.H.* pp. 42, 71.
[2] *M.E.* I. p. 177.
[3] *R.I.* p. 145.

destruction but as the supreme act which consecrates his entire life and in which he reaches self-fulfilment.[1] It is, in this sense, that we can speak of the personal act as creative and of the person as self-creative in his activity. Personal activity, in the sense not simply of the activity of someone but of activity in which a person is present in the full meaning we have found for that word, is creative both because it is not essentially productive of – though it may, as instance artistic creativity, be realised through the production of some identifiable object – and because what it brings into being – the person that in so acting I become – can never be precisely or specifically foreseen.[2]

What is essential in the creator is the act by which he places himself at the disposition of something which, doubtless, in a certain sense depends upon him in order to be, but which, at the same time, is presented to him as beyond what he judges himself capable of drawing forth directly and immediately from within himself ... How can we help recognizing that the person is inconceivable outside the act by which he creates himself but, at the same time, that this act is in some manner suspended from an order that surpasses him?[3]

In the light of these reflections upon the meaning of presence, value, and activity in the personal context, we can better understand the meaning of freedom. "The problem of freedom, the real problem... can itself only be stated on a certain spiritual level ... Freedom is only possible in the measure of my having within me the means by which I can transcend the order of the *him*."[4] "The opposition between a philosophy of being and a philosophy of freedom cannot be maintained."[5] "The free act is essentially a significant act ... What distinguishes the free act is that it helps to make me what I am, ... whereas the contingent or insignificant act, the act which might just as well be performed by anybody, has no contribution to make to this sort of creation of myself by myself: to that extent it can scarcely be considered as an act."[6] That the person is essentially free has already been implicit in the recognition that it is only within recollection, which he is at liberty to adopt or not adopt, that he can become aware of and acknowledge his personal status and, equally, promote the value inherent in that status. The recognition escapes the charge of circularity precisely because it *is* recognition and not argument by deductive or inductive inference from objective propositions. The various reflected aspects of that initial and

[1] *R.I.* p. 106; *M.E.* I. p. 181.
[2] *H.V.* p. 31; *P.E.* p. 114; *M.E.* II. p. 118.
[3] *H.V.* p. 31.
[4] *J.M.* pp. 204, 215.
[5] *P.I.* p. 20.
[6] *M.E.* II. pp. 117, 118.

comprehensive recognition certainly reinforce each other's value and sharpen the focus of the initial recognition itself; but, since each is metaproblematic only in the context of that recognition, they both derive from it their value and maintain it only within its continuing context. As Marcel justly remarks:

Freedom can only be thought by freedom, it creates or constitutes itself in its thinking of itself. There is a sort of circle here that reflect on has to recognize and which has about it nothing vicious. The idea of a freedom that would demonstrate itself or which one could make emerge from a dialectical determinism is a pseudo-idea whose contradiction reflection shows.[1]

So thought, the element of choice takes on a secondary significance in the understanding of the concept of the person as free. Certainly, it is part of that concept that the person should be free in his actual choosing to do this or that action and in his active recognition of his personal value. To say that this freedom may be limited by the factors either external or internal to himself that lie beyond his control is no contradiction of this fact. The possibility is already implicit in the concept of the person as being situate and existing embodied, supported by the recognition of the essential non-invariancy of his presence together with that of the alienation inherent in genuine having. The recognition of the person as presence, however, forbids the conclusion that he is necessarily so determined in all his choices. One may, indeed, find it difficult to argue one's way out of the dialectical maze of determinism from the purely problematic standpoint, but it is equally impossible from that standpoint to establish its universal validity. Support for, at least, the possibility of the metaproblematic view of freedom in choice – and indirectly of the account we have given of creative activity – even comes from psycho-analysis. The very fact that one can discover the hidden forces secretly at work within the psyche, argues the possibility of an extension of freedom's scope.[2] Insofar as it suggests that we might be less free and less often that unreflectively we had thought, it is already catered for in Marcel's concept of the person as embodied presence. Even here, Marcel's assertion that the person in situation can confront it and assume its responsibility as he might that of his own act, shows how what is more passive in ourselves can be activitated by participation in the active principle of our being. By being limited, our freedom is not obliterated and by recognizing our limitations, we can in some measure effectively transcend them, precisely by assuming them within our

[1] *P.I.* p. 20.
[2] C.f. Nuttin, *op. cit.* pp. 138ff; Hampshire, *op. cit.* pp. 178–180.

freedom. We might remark, too, in this connection, what little real relevance there is in the question of the predictability of our actions. Certainly, again, a person who is physically or psychologically crippled may in fact be entirely predictable in his actions to someone with sufficient knowledge of his patterns of behaviour; but insofar as he is thus determined, he cannot be said to be acting *qua* person, in the sense in which we have found to be that of personal activity as such. This is not to deny him any personal status, but to recognise that such status involves an exigency for being more – and, therefore, personally – whose fulfilment is not automatically guaranteed.[1] On the other hand, the saint who, in the light of what has been said of value and of what shall yet be said of freedom, can well be regarded as of mortal men the most free, may be quite as predictable in his actions – to someone that is who understands the meaning of sanctity and can truly appreciate what in a given situation it requires of action. There is withal a sense in which no free act is predictable and this is not that of its happening. For, while it is true that a free act can be more or less consciously assumed and deliberately orientated, its actual value as free act is something which will hardly be appreciated except *a posteriori*: "there is no doubt that it is something which reflection will recognize as a value, rather than a sort of immediate evidence accompanying the act at the actual moment of its performance."[2] This arises from the fact not only that the full consequences of my action are *de facto* impossible to assess before I have acted and while I am acting, or that even the saint is conscious of never quite being adequate to the ontological value whose promise he bears within him, but also that this value is of its nature objectively in-specifiable. "We should never forget that my position is such that I cannot rightly know who I am and who I shall be."[3] And this recalls attention to the creative nature of the free act and to the deeper meaning of being free from which concentration upon freedom of choice, freedom *to*, distracts us. Freedom in its deepest sense is not merely freedom *to* but such in order to be freedom *for*.

The idea that freedom essentially consists in freedom to choose probably derives from a confusion of desire with will and from a mistaken emphasis on autonomy. To want, in the sense of will, is not to desire. This is witnessed to by the concrete experience of my being able to want what is in fact clean contrary to my desires and by the further

---

[1] Once again, we must enter a *caveat*. The frustration of personal development indicated holds only for this world.
[2] *M.E.* II. p. 118.
[3] *Ibid.*

fact that most often it is in carrying this will through to action that I am most conscious of being free. Not that this entails that willing be a joyless exercise of grim determination. In fact, the more I succeed in controlling my desires and in schooling my will to the pursuit of the truly valuable, the more of grace and ease appears in my activity. On the other hand, the more my wanting succumbs to the seduction of my desires, the quicker they become compulsions. And this but recognizes once again the possessive nature of desire already discerned in the earlier stages of our inquiry.[1] A further feature of willing now emerges with bearing on the nature of my personal freedom. Willing, insofar as it is opposed to desire, involves a refusal to calculate possibilities or, at least, suspends such calculation.[2] The more effective my willing – the more, that is, it is willing – the more integrated my activity and the more complete my committal. This points to a total commitment in freedom that goes beyond any objectively specifiable value. That is freedom is essentially an orientation to what transcends my present self; but it is equally an active assumption of the exigency for being in which any particular movement of transcendance moves and in whose value it participates insofar as it is of value. "No act of committal is possible except for a being who can be distinguished from his own momentary situation and who *recognizes* this difference between himself and his situation and consequently treats himself as somehow transcending his own life-process, and answers for himself.[3] This, in turn, makes clear another mistake involved the equation of freedom with *"liberté d'indifference."* For, that concept implies that what is at stake in personal activity is insignificant, whereas in fact freedom in the full sense only comes into play where the stake is of real importance – which, in the final analysis, means where it is I myself who am at stake: "I must realize *in concreto* that I should be betraying or denying myself if I failed to set this value on the stake."[4] My freedom, then, derives its deepest significance – the significance that makes the free act *the* significant act – from its assumption of my destiny. To recognise my destiny as mine involves a twofold acknowledgement: that my destiny is only mine in being assumed consciously and freely by me and that as my destiny and assumed by me it is inscribed in my existing as its exigency and, therefore, is not something which derives its meaning and its value from my assuming it so much as it is something from which in its assumption I derive my

[1] *M.E.* II. p. 112.
[2] *Ibid.*
[3] *B.H.* p. 42.
[4] *M.E.* II. p. 117; c.f. *P.I.* p. 23.

meaning and my value. If, then, in the final analysis, "to say: I am free, is to say: I am myself," this affirmation must be counterbalanced by the assertion: "freedom has an aim assigned to it, and that aim is salvation."[1]

In this context, the idea that freedom is essentially autonomy loses its significance. In the first place, it is contradicted by the creative character of my freedom. Autonomy only has significance in a context where there is something to be administered and, as such, belongs to the category of having. That is to say, I can speak of my autonomy only with respect to something over which I can and have to exercise control; but nothing in my life or my presence, insofar as they are mine, admits of this concept being applied. My life and my activity are the more mine, the more I commit myself in them, as we have seen, and "the more I enter into the whole of an activity with the whole of myself the less is it legitimate to say that I am autonomous.[2] In this respect, the only thing under my strict control is whether or not I will *accept* my onto-logical destiny.[3] This means that the notion of freedom as autonomy is further contradicted in whatever sense it has of asserting me as the origin and source of values. Apart from the fact, which we have already been led to recognize, that the person *qua* valuable transcends any specific evaluation made of him or any value yet realized in his activity, the value to which he can ultimately aspire is itself recognisable as such only as participating in Being. The self that enters as creator of values can only be the empirical self – for the theory in effect denies any transcendence – so that these values are by definition problematic and as such correspond, as Marcel points out, to less-being.[4] So much is this the case, that outside the metaproblematic recognition of the person, any action will inevitably appear as a limitation of the possibilities that were mine before acting. Personal activity escapes that limitation only by its insertion in the fundamental reference of my being to Being; nonetheless, as we saw the case to be with the saint, I am always conscious of never adequately measuring up to the promise I carry within me. "The person grasps himself less as being than as will to surpass what at once he is and is not – an actuality in which he feels himself to be involved or implicated, but which does not satisfy him: which does not measure up to the aspiration with which he is identified

---

[1] *M.E.* II. p. 115; *B.H.* p. 80; *R.I.* p. 45.
[2] *B.H.* p. 173.
[3] C.f. *H.P.* p. 71.
[4] C.f. *H.P.* pp. 49–50.

– his device is not *sum*, but *sursum*."[1] While it is true, therefore, that the person can only realize himself in the act through which he tends to incarnate himself – "in a work, an action, an entire life" – it is of his essence never to crystallize himself definitively in any particular incarnation. "That is the profound reason why it is impossible to think the person or the personal order, without, at the same time, thinking what is beyond both, a suprapersonal reality that presides over all his initiatives, that is at once his principle and his end."[2]

In what measure one should feel called upon and, if so, in what measure one could feel able to pronounce upon the nature of such a reality within the limits of this present inquiry, we shall leave until its close. The point made, we think, is well made. For, between the assertion that all values issue from one's own determination of and the affirmation of their transcendent source – however one is to conceive it – implicit in the recognition that one's own rôle is their recognition, there seems to be no third position. And in the final analysis, to assert the first proposition is both to contradict the general and traditional belief of men as well to reduce all values to a purely subjective status which allows of their contradiction by whomsover chooses to do so. Nor does there seem any real escape in the assertion of the social origin of values. Society as such is a mere abstraction like the transcendental ego. What exist are particular societies whose values, however determined, have exactly the force of their being the values of the individual persons who form that society and whose acceptance individually invests its values with authority. That is to say, freedom transcends heteronomy as much as it transcends the autonomy with which it is necessarily contrasted. Only within the recognition of a common participation in a reality which transcends it can a society be rightly deemed a locus of value. Its values, however, are still subject to the same metaproblematic criticism to which are subject the individual person's. They withstand objective criticism in the same sense as do the values to which the individual person adheres. That is to say, the values which a society professes are valuable in the measure that they represent the common agreement of its members in their several recognitions of their common destiny as persons. The danger, here, as in the individual person's case, lies in the operation of what Marcel has termed "the spirit of abstraction." Here, it works through the reification of a society, in abstraction from the persons whose mutual presence and creative activity

[1] *H.V.* p. 32.
[2] *H.V.* pp. 32–33.

vivify it, as a collectivity. In opposition to the collectivity and the
fanaticism it breeds to sustain itself, "the individual, but inasmuch as
he is bearer of universal values" – which, as we have seen, are equally
and finally personal values – "can set himself up... upholding true
justice, thereby understanding one affirmed as true against the pretend-
ed and false justice which society intends to impose." Neither can we
argue that the individual merely anticipates a social order yet to be
established which, incidentally, would be called upon to reverse any
condemnation of him by the contemporary order against which he has
set himself. For, the very recognition of the possibility of an evolving
social moral consciousness – and there is no reason to deny this fact
within limits – implies a trans-social value which any given human
society, like any individual person, can betray and only inadequately
embody in its specific values.

It is not, evidently, the simple distinction of time before and time after on which we
can hope to found anything that resembles a judgment of value. We can only hope
to get out of this inextricable situation by declaring that the individual prophet is the
bearer of a certain message translating a transcendent rtuth... This means to say
that the value in question can only be recognized by a regard which is not orientated
along a purely temporal axis, along a line simply linking up a before and after.[1]

Nonetheless, society – in its authentic sense of a communion of persons
qua persons – remains the necessary milieu in which alone I can work
out my personal salvation – that is, my ontological fulfilment *qua*
person. "I tend to affirm myself as person in the measure in which,
assuming the responsibility of my acts, I behave as a real being, participating in a real society."[2] Such a real society is a function of the self-
creativity of the persons who within it co-operate in and contribute to
each other's creativity: authentic society is a mutual creativity of
authentic persons. For this reason, there is justice in Marcel's mistrust
of the efficacy of mass movements in effecting the conversion of a group
of individuals into an authentic community of persons. "It must be
understood that universality is situated in the dimension of depth and
not in that of extension."[3] Thus, while "there is authentic depth only
where a community can be effectively realised; it will never be either
among individuals centred on themselves, and consequently sclerosed,
or in the bosom of the mass, in its state of being a mass": "any effective
approach to being has as its condition the return to the neighbour" and

[1] *H.P.* pp. 39–41; c.f. also *H.C.H.* Part II. Chap. 2.
[2] *H.V.* p. 27.
[3] *H.C.H.* p. 202.

it is, therefore, "only within groups fairly restricted in size and animated by a spirit of love that the universal can really be embodied."[1]

It is in the presence of other persons recognized as such and by contributing to the sustenance and deepening of that presence that the person can effectively sustain and deepen his own presence in himself. The converse equally holds. This, in effect, is what his freedom is *for*. We must then examine the modes in which this mutual presence of persons is actively recognized and, at the same time, in the effective recognition created. We must also take note of the obstacles which such a recognition encounters and how it can be said to overcome them. For, its is in such encounters, which he terms "*ordeals*," that Marcel sees the real test of presence and not in abstract argument about the terms in which the experience of presence is expressed without relation to the fundamental situations from which those terms derive their meaning and their relevance.[2] "At the basis of ordeal," Marcel observes, "we find a questioning of immediate experience... The proper function of ordeal is to make possible a reflected judgment that allows of qualifying, with respect to the real, the immediate affirmation made at the outset."[3] It is, moreover, of the essence of ordeal that it may not be recognized as such and this, not only in the sense of my not facing up to its implications, but equally in the sense of my yielding in face of it, finding in it an excuse for abandoning the affirmation which ordeal challenges me to uphold. In this sense, ordeal is as much a testing of myself as it a means of clarifying for me the meaning of what I am. For, we do not speak of ordeal – even in the context of submitting to the test of time – except in connection with something that is of real value. Real value, as we have seen, involves an intimate bond between what is valued and what is supremely valuable in me and, therefore, in the strict and full sense, personal. In this light, too, life becomes an ordeal, the ordeal with reference to which any other takes on its character of ordeal. I am at stake. The question thus becomes one of inquiring into the modes in which I can affirm my presence as person – and with that the presence of those I love – in face of the various ways in which such presence threatens to dissolve in absence, more or less complete. Perhaps the most concrete form in which life appears as ordeal is as involving death. If the basic answer to the challenge preferred by ordeal is *fidelity* – "Being as the place of fidelity"[4] – fidelity itself involves and is maintained

[1] *H.C.H.* pp. 200, 202.
[2] C.f. *P.I.* pp. 25–26.
[3] *R.I.* pp. 101–102.
[4] *B.H.* p. 41.

along those concrete approaches to the person: *belief, hope, love*. These can be seen as ways in which fidelity is maintained in the face of the scepticism, despair, and complete rejection which in the face of the ordeal which life and, in particular, death present account the enduring reality of personal presence nonsensical, of no value, simply absent.

Fidelity, in the context of Marcel's philosophy and the concept of the person this involves, is essentially the service of a free man. In this it presents an interesting contrast with moral theories based upon a concept of duty as representing the supreme moral value. Fidelity, however, is a concept quite distinct from that of obedience. Obedience is, primarily what one exacts from a child, precisely because he lacks the powers of reasoning and the experience to decide for himself what to do. It would be absurd to demand obedience in this sense from an adult. It is true, nonetheless, that there are situations, certain sectors of his life in which an adult has to obey. Obedience, in this context, however, is not the same thing as being obedient. It is the act by which one replies to that of the chief who is in command, whose function is to command, as it is that of his subordinate to obey. Since it is a question of function, the duty of obedience does not necessarily or deeply commit the being of the person who obeys. The obligation only bears upon the specific actions which he is obliged to perform or from which he is obliged to abstain, whatever his personal feelings or the personal character of his chief. Obedience goes out to the chief as chief, that is to the function and not to the man. Where the personal quality of the chief comes into play, and in the exact measure that it does, or where there is something of personal adherence vivifying obedience, it takes on the character of fidelity. Obedience, as fidelity cannot be, is commanded. Furthermore, its frontiers, as those of fidelity cannot be, must strictly be defined; for, in the absence of such definition, obedience degenerates into servility. It is equally clear that where obedience is rendered out of love it is quite transposed into the key of fidelity.[1]

It can be clearly seen from this that obedience, since it is in essence functional, presupposes the non-functional service of fidelity in order to be itself of value. Even in a completely servile state, where everybody enjoys a purely functional status – in order to maintain which anything resembling freedom is prudently discouraged – somewhere, at the locus of authority, somehow, if only in caricature, something resembling fidelity is invoked. The leadership, be it individual or collective, claims authority either in virtue of purely idosyncratic fidelity to itself

[1] C.f. *H.V.* pp. 171–172, 176–177.

or in virtue of being the faithful interpreter and voice of a transcendent
source of authority which is invested with some of the attributes of the
person and which is presumed to be indefectibly faithful to itself. We can
see, then, how the concept of fidelity is involved in the question of how
the common presence of persons *qua* person can be sustained without
either dissolving into sheer anarchy or being stifled by tyranny however
paternal in aspect. And this can only be by recognizing in fidelity a
fidelity to oneself as person, indissociably linked to a fidelity to one's
fellows as persons, in common recognition of a common participation
in a reality which, while founding each as absolutely valuable with
respect to one another, transcends in value each and all of them. This
value, as Marcel clearly states, whether considered in its transcendent
reality or in its participative presence in individual persons can be
neither a principle nor a mere idea. To conceive of it as mere principle
is to confuse constancy – which may indeed be a necessary framework
for fidelity – with fidelity itself. Constancy could be defined as the fact
of persevering in a certain project. The project as such, however, is
impersonal and whether it concern myself or others, leaves no room for
what precisely is personal in me or them. This element, presence, re-
enters once I think of constancy in the personal context – of a faithful
friend. A faithful friend is someone who does not fail me, who resists the
test of circumstances; so far is he from absenting himself that I always
find him there *with* me in adversity. It is this word *with* that shows how
far the constancy of a friend is removed from that of someone who
perseveres in a project to assist me, or adheres to an *idea* that he has
formed of himself as someone who does not let other people down.[1]
There is here, in this *being with* – which reveals the presence of a friend
who regards me as a person and not merely as an occasion for the flexing
of his moral muscles –, the same total commitment that alone can make
sense of my fidelity to my promise. The difficulty there confronting us
is that the oath of fidelity seems to be made on the basis of a certain
inward disposition which, with the passage of time, may alter. How
can I commit myself to acting as if this change were not liable to occur?
And yet to refuse committal on such grounds would make all social life
impossible. More importantly the refusal is based on certain miscon-
ceptions bearing, precisely, on the nature of the person. The first is that
at any given moment I am identified completely with the state in which
I can at that moment objectively establish myself to be. The second is
that my future state is something that will happen in the manner of an

[1] *R.I.* pp. 205–213; *B.H.* pp. 48–53.

external event. Our previous inquiry has shown the fallacy in each. We may conclude, then, that when I commit myself, I posit in principle that the commitment will not be called in question. Furthermore, it is clear that this active willing itself intervenes as an essential factor in determining what shall happen.[1] In this light, we can see that fidelity is creative, in the same way that the free and personal act in which it is embodied was said to be creative. In being faithful to my fellow, I actively conserve his presence in its personal reality, not as image or mere object. In my fidelity to him, I continually recreate my presence to myself and fulfil in the renewing my being. "Faithfulness is, in reality, the exact opposite of inert conformism. It is the active recognition of something permanent, not formally, after the manner of a law, but ontologically; in this sense, it refers invariably to a presence, or to something which can be maintained within and before us as a presence, but which, *ipso facto*, can just as well be ignored, forgotten and obliterated; and this reminds of the menace of betrayal which… overshadows our whole world."[2]

The concept of the person, then, emerges as the concept of a presence indefectible insofar as it is the active recognition of its co-participation in a communion of presence which it ever lies within its power to betray but, equally, which it is its peculiar destiny to sustain. "Creative fidelity consists in maintaining ourselves actively in a permeable state; and there is a mysterious interchange between this free act and the gift granted in response to it."[3] So little then is the concept of person a closed concept – the concept of a reality imprisoned within itself in monadic solitude – that the greatest obstacle to a person's realisation of the ideal it signifies is self-encumbrance. "To be incapable of presence is to be in some manner not only occupied but encumbered with one's own self."[4] The preoccupation may be immediately with something I should not identify myself with. The preoccupation, that is, is not so much a matter of being occupied with a *particular object* as being occupied in a *particular manner*. How this should be, we have already seen in our earlier consideration of the significance of having. It is equally true that the more the world is thought according to the category informed by the possessive attitude, the more it appears hostile to the very possibility of presence. *Disponibilité* – a term very inadequately conveyed by "availability," even if qualified by "total spiritual" – disponibility is

[1] *R.I.* pp. 205–213; *B.H.* pp. 48–53.
[2] *P.E.* pp. 21–22.
[3] *P.E.* p. 24.
[4] *P.E.* p. 27.

the moral attitude corresponding to the intellectual attitude we have termed metaproblematic. Just as indisponibility is rooted in some measure in alienation – from myself, from others, from being –, so disponibility is rooted in an active intimacy. Inquiry into the fundamental modes in which the presence of others is recognised – and therefore in which fidelity is affirmed – will likewise be, therefore, an inquiry into the fundamental attitudes that dispose the person to the active fostering of their personal reality and the whole process of its fulfilment.[1]

"If creative fidelity is conceivable," Marcel asserts, "it is because fidelity is ontological in its principle, because it prolongs presence which itself corresponds to a certain kind of hold which being has on us; because it multiplies and deepens the effect of this presence almost unfathomably in our lives."[2] It may well be asked of what nature is the affirmation of presence on which fidelity is founded and which it is called upon to maintain. Marcel's answer is that it is belief. There are we think good grounds for this assertion but, equally, that what is being asserted must be carefully understood, The belief in question is quite distinct from the kind of belief we might think involved in asserting, on the problematic level of reflection, the "existence" of the objects specified by objective description. In the first place, we must distinguish between opinion, conviction, and belief. In general, opinion may be said to be concerned with the unknown. This lack of knowledge need not, however, be either self-evident or admitted. Opinion, in fact, wavers between a mere impression and an assertion. It runs through the whole gamut lying between a *seeming so* and a *claiming that*. The more an opinion has to be maintained against another, the more it pretends to be a claiming. Here, we must distinguish between the essentially impure opinion, – views at secondhand involving a self-identification with the anonymous '*on*' – and an opinion embodying an element of ideal justification which, Marcel sees in assertions or denials from within the problematic that claim a universal validity. These involve a *hyperdoxal* element that is irreducible to the Platonic *doxa*. In particular, in the denial of the metaproblematic, there is a claim to a double verification negative and positive. Negatively, it consists in the claim that if the subject of problematic assertion existed, the claimant would have perceived it. Positively, it consist in the claim, expressed or unexpressed, to the possession of a corpus of facts with which the

[1] C.f. *P.E.* pp. 23–28.
[2] *P.E.* p. 23.

metaproblematically affirmed is incompatible. The important thing about such a claim is its reduction of a reality pertaining to an order distinct from that to which belong the "facts" with which it is declared to be incompatible. This leads us to distinguish another attitude midway between opinion and belief: conviction. The fact of being *convinced that* presents the character of adopting a definitive position. In professing a conviction, I assert a conclusion that I have come to as preferable to any other. The affirmation, however, relates not merely to the immutability of my inward disposition: it extends, by way of judgment, arbitrarily or no, to bear upon the object itself. We have already seen, in connection with fidelity, the extreme difficulty in maintaining such a claim. It is not clear by what right I could affirm the immutability of the dispositional complex itself.[1]

This brings us to belief. Its attitude is, precisely, that of fidelity. Unlike the 'closed' attitude informing opinion and conviction, its attitude is essentially 'open.' That is to say, belief opens a credit in favour of what or, rather, whom I *believe in*. In other words, belief is essentially a matter of *believing in* not of *believing that*: the more, in fact, I translate this *believing in* into terms of *believing that*, the more my belief takes on the character of conviction. Belief is, in fact, a committal, not only with regard to what *I have* but with regard to what *I am*, to what I believe in. From this point of view, "the strongest belief, or more exactly the most living, is that which absorbs most fully all the powers of your being." It is obvious that its focus can only be the personal or what, in affirming the person, appears as super-personal. It is obvious too, that belief carries with it an assurance of the same order as existential assurance, going beyond what is objectively given, and that it is equally liable to eclipse: my belief can degenerate into an opinion. It is equally obvious that belief as such cannot be approached except from within the situation which evokes it.[1] What Marcel is doing here, in effect, is indicating the character of metaproblematic affirmation, radically distinguishing it from problematic assertion, and assigning as its context the personal as such. In the light of our previous investigations he is quite justified in so doing. His action is supported both by the cognitive and the affective features of metaproblematic as contrasted with problematic discourse, which we found to be inherent in any conception of language as a means of communication between persons in a common existential situation and directed to the clarification of that situation. Discourse within that

[1] *M.E.* II. pp. 69–78; *R.I.* pp. 161–175.
[2] *M.E.* II. pp. 77–81.

situation, abstracting from the fundamental situation itself, and controlled by interests arising within it – as indeed any interest by definition must – but abstracting from the total interest which the situation itself presents for recognition – and which can therefore be ignored, taken for granted or denied – is informed by an attitude quite other than that of *believing in*. In such discourse identification is purely a practical matter of defining the interest in function of which the various topics or 'particulars' are going to be described. Strictly speaking, the *ipseities* which, on the level of metaproblematic reflection, we can *believe in*, on the problematic level only appear, if at all, on the periphery of the universe of any particular discourse. The particulars that do appear in any generalised version of such a universe of discourse – itself a *type* – do so only as variables, as *types* therefore to be instanced. Here, we must interject, that our analysis is phenomenological and neither psychological nor logical.[1] In such discourse I cannot talk of the *ipseities* I believe in, *as such*. Strictly speaking, I myself *qua* myself do not inhabit that universe. (This may be what was at the back of such opinions as that the 'I' in "I have a toothache" is different in its use from the 'I' in "I've got a bad tooth"). In such a universe, moreover, emotion is either bracketted or objectivized, when, for reasons already touched upon, it ceases to be emotion. And this bracketting or objectivization is not necessarily "emotive": it only become such when the divorce is made absolute and used to deny any reality to emotion. Similarly, the "particulars" I admit as basic to the conceptual scheme used as frame of reference in such discourse may well – it would be odd if it did not ever, since the universe itself is abstracted from the universe I exist in – coincide with the *ipseities* I can believe in. (When I act, they necessarily do, since effective action closes the problematic gap, as Marcel has shown: a further confirmation that our being overflows our awareness and our awareness, our language). When I speak of them, as the *ipseities* they are, whether I am aware of it or not, my attitude has changed and all the meaning involved in that change comes into play. It is a different game. Quite naturally, too, emotion ceases to be excluded – as Marcel remarks, "emotion functions as a recall": "emotion makes me come into, the scene, it forces the hidden *me* to emerge."[2]

[1] "Phenomenological analysis" can here be taken as an analysis of the meaning of concepts with reference to the existential situation that evokes them. If we said that what they refer to "appears" this means in this context "is manifest." "Appears" is not contrasted with "is the case." Neither is it a question of contrasting "seeming to be" with "really being": It is a question of recognizing what presents itself for recognition.

[2] *J.M.* p. 172; c.f. Hillman, *op. cit.* pp. 257–258, on emotion as "symbolic apprehension of the world."

In belief, however, there is no room for the divorce between the cognitive and affective aspects of awareness that objective thought operates. It is not an "impression" *plus* a "belief" in the "emotive" sense. It is an affirmation in which I am totally involved of a reality totally affirmed. As appendix to this account, we may observe, that, while metaproblematic affirmation affirms impersonal and personal existing alike *as* existing, metaproblematic reflection is unable to proceed with the clarification of impersonal existing in the same sympathetic way in which it can in the case of persons. My awareness of impersonal existing is limited, as we have already noted, to the awareness of a common, though unequal, participation in Being. What might be that degree remains as much unknown as mysterious. It could only be thought by very distant analogy with personal existing. *Believing in* is, as Marcel rightly asserts, a believing in persons *qua* persons. The conclusion is forced upon us that any denial of the metaproblematic from a problematic standpoint is indeed an opinion imbued with a *hyperdoxal* element, however much it be stated as conviction. From that standpoint, the metaproblematic can neither be affirmed nor denied. From the other standpoint, affirmation is by way of recognition, nor could it be otherwise.

The credit opened by *believing in*, brings us to the question of hope. Once again, the concept must be approached in the light of the meaning it enjoys in its strongest use, which is precisely that relevant to our inquiry, in a truly personal context. In dilution, hope may indicate nothing more vital than a wish, with nothing very much at stake. We recall that value is manifest, and in strict proportion, when something is at stake and most strongly as personal value, *the* valuable by participation, when it is we ourselves who are in jeopardy. "Hope in its strongest form is directed towards a salvation."[1] For this reason its context is metaproblematic. In the problematic world, strictly speaking, nothing is at stake; although in the metaproblematic world from which the former is abstracted what was the object of purely problematic interest and, even, the whole process of inquiry itself may well become of personal concern. One rôle of emotion, existentially conceived, is, as we saw, precisely to recall that personal concern; but, quite rightly, on entering the problematic sphere, emotion and with it personal involvement are left behind. And this is only to stress once more the strictly functional nature of all problematic inquiry, be it practical or theoretical, and its dependence on the non-functional personal order

[1] *H.V.* p. 40.

for its value. Thus, for brief example, we quite rightly expect a surgeon to banish personal considerations in his actual surgery: they would not help and might well hinder it. Not that the personal approach is out of place, once the operation is concluded and the whole person, not just the area abstracted for surgical incision, becomes the subject of concern. Nor that the objective work of surgery itself is without value, but this precisely is because of its relevance to the person operated on. The surgeon himself participates in the world of personal values through his personal concern for his patient. It was precisely the lack of such personal concern that ultimately made possible and, in the event, constituted the obscenity of those experiments upon living persons which took place in certain concentration camps.[1] The digression is not irrelevant to the point at present issue. For, it is only within the strictly personal context, as subject of personal concern and not as object of technical or clinical interest, that the person is subject of hope, in the twofold sense of subject. For, *qua* metaproblematic, hoping is a way of being present that the involves the subject hoped for and the subject hoping for *as* persons.

In the first place, hope must not be confused with optimism. The optimist is someone with the firm conviction, or, in its weaker form, the vague sentiment that "things are going to turn out alright." The vagueness of "things" is not accidental. Although optimism can vary in degree and form, the differences between its various forms and degrees is not so deep as might be imagined, for optimism is not really profound. In the last analysis, the optimist always finds his support in an experience, which, far from being intensely lived or intimately grasped, is viewed from *sufficient a distance* to enable certain oppositions it presents to attenuate or fuse in a general harmony.[2] Hope, on the other hand, is called into play in situations wherein life is experienced as hard captivity: "I appear to myself as captive when I find myself not merely cast into, but, as it were, involved in, by way of external constraint, a mode of existing that is imposed upon me and brings with it restrictions of every kind upon my personal activity."[3] The more this captivity is personally experienced, however, the more it appears to share in the quality of a frustration of my whole being, whose most intense and ultimate pitch is death. My own death is a question easily shelved; it is the death of those I cherish that presents the *ordeal* in which hope is

[1] C.f. *D.W.* pp. 1–20 *passim.*
[2] *H.V.* pp. 45–46.
[3] *H.V.* p. 41.

most severely and finally challenged. In my own case, it is more often in the experience of my captive self – in which my very being seems frustrated in its most intimate, profound, and meaningful development – that I most nearly share in the menace of utter dissolution of presence that the death of my friend seems to offer. It is in such situations that I am called upon to resist the fatal fascination which the *idea* of my own or my friend's destruction exerts to the point of inviting my capitulation before its *fatum* and so the anticipation in spirit of that destruction itself.[1] The contrast with this refusal, literally, to *unmake* myself is provided by *despair*, not fear. Fear is the correlate of desire and, like it, pertains to the category of having. Its object is always in some way conceived in the manner of a prized possession that is being wrested from my grasp or from my control. This remains true even where I may be truly said to fear for my life and explains how it is the martyr – whatever be that to which by his self-sacrifice he testifies as supremely valuable – can, while fearing death, overcome the desire to maintain his corporeal existence in the assurance of his hope that thereby he will, somehow, live on.[2] But, precisely, this living on is not – at least its subject's and by him so conceived – here and now. That is to say, that while hope has no illusions, such as nourish mere optimism, it can lay no claim on any technique to secure its fulfilment.

Every technique serves, or can be made to serve, some desire or some fear; conversely, every desire as every fear tends to invent its appropriate technique. From this standpoint, despair consists in the recognition of the ultimate inefficacy of all technics, joined to the inability or the refusal to change over to a new ground – a ground where all technics are seen to be incompatible with the fundamental nature of being, and which itself escapes our grasp (insofar as our grasp is limited to the world of objects and of things).[3]

Hoping, that is, invincibly tends to transcend the particular objects to which at first it might seem to be attached. It is a case of *hoping in*, not of *hoping that*.[4] It is important to inquire closely into the meaning of this. Hoping does not bear upon events or upon the means whereby such events may be effected in any problematic sense. As Marcel asserts, it is beyond all calculations and reckoning up of possibilities.[5] Whatever eventuality is hoped for is so hoped for on behalf of some person, myself or other. But, obviously, there is nothing in hoping for such eventuality that of itself gives any assurance that it will take place. The formula of

[1] *H.V.* pp. 48–50.
[2] *R.I.* p. 106.
[3] *P.E.* p. 18.
[4] *H.V.* pp. 43–60, 75.
[5] *B.H.* p. 79.

hoping, if any were at all adequate, would be: "As before, but otherwise and better than before."[1] Now, this cannot be understood outside the personal context. That is, just as despair is ultimately a complete abandonment of faith in any enduring value or reality, hope "makes appeal to the existence of a certain creativity in the world, or again to real resources placed at the disposal of this creativity."[2] That is to say, hoping is essentially *in* the indefectibility of personal presence as participating in Being, itself indefectible. It bears on any hoped for event only as necessarily bound up with the indefectibility of such presence and this latter is something of which it is not sure. That is to say, the hope for any such eventuality is always conditional upon its actually being involved in the presence unconditionally affirmed as indefectible. What this latter affirmation might mean is best approached in the light of the ordeal presented by death.

What does it mean to hope in the face of the death of someone I love? Quite simply it means to affirm their continued presence, even though they have ceased to exist. As Marcel puts it through the mouth of a character in one of his plays: "To love someone is to say: You shall not die."[3] But what does this mean? It might mean that I swear to keep within me their memory as a living presence, to understand what this means is already to see that something more is implied. For as presence, even in memory, the person is not an object. The faithful memory maintains the affirmation of presence that fidelity and belief made during the dead person's life. "To consent to the death of a being is in some sense to deliver him over to death."[4] To accept the total dissolution of the presence that the person is means that one in fact denies that he ever was a person: that is, a reality that transcends the purely physical. Now, while hope, in this context, appears as the affirmation of the continued presence of the person after death – and not merely within the memory of his friends – the foundation of its assurance is precisely the central reality of the person whose continued presence is affirmed – to which the faithful memory is a witness – a presence that, as participative in Being, was affirmed in the existential affirmation, the affirmation of personal value, the recognition of personal creativity, and prolonged in fidelity and belief. Its value is no way doubtful as might be a particular event hoped for on his behalf, since it concerns him totally *qua* person. Negatively, this assurance is strengthened by the recognition

[1] *H.V.* p. 90.
[2] *H.V.* p. 69.
[3] In *Le Mort de Demain*.
[4] *H.V.* p. 205.

that there can be no question of treating the disappearance of a person from the visible world as final. There is no logical proof that death is final. For, though it is difficult to understand, much less imagine, what presence, after death might be; there is nothing in the human condition to support its extinction, even problematically conceived – since the person as such, as we have seen, in no way falls *qua person* within the competence of problematic thought; while from the metaproblematic standpoint this continued presence, with all it implies, impels our *recognition*. Survival, then, but what of immortality? Immortality, for Marcel, means more than mere survival of disembodied presence – which, in the full sense he gives the term, is not existing, although it still signifies what is most important in being human – but exis ting once more – "as before, though otherwise and better." That is to say, the issue in question is the resurrection of the body – a strictly non-philosophical question. On this question, philosophy – problematic or metaproblematic – can say, for or against, precisely nothing.[1]

"Hoping is essentially, it can be said, the disponibility of a soul intimately enough committed in an experience of communion in order to accomplish the act transcending willing and knowing whereby it affirms the living perennity of which this experience offers at once the pledge and the first fruits."[2]

In the light of all that has been said, the "definition" is clear and well made. It sufficiently marks the fact that hoping, like fidelity and be- lieving, is creative in the contribution it makes to the recognition – cogni- tive, affective, and effective – of presence. We have seen that presence in order to be sustained as presence requires the perpetual renewal of its recognition, all at once passive and active, in fidelity, to which hopes gives it motive power and faith its intelligible frame. But presence so faithfully sustained is presence completely accepted and this is love in which, traditionally, all other virtues have their source and in which they all come home. Speaking of the distinctive propositions that could be said to have emerged with the conclusion of his inquiry into the Mystery of Being in his Gifford Lectures, Marcel asserts: "The most important of these propositions consists, I think, in asserting philoso- phically, (that is to say short of any theological specification) the

---

[1] C.f. *P.I.* pp. 181–193; *H.V.* pp. 189–214: "not existing" in this context does *not* mean "no longer being." Marcel's most apt expression of what might this after-life is through the lips of Arnaud Chartrain, a charter in his play, *La Soif*, Desclée de Brouwer, Paris 1938: "Through death we open ourselves to what we have lived on earth."
[2] *H.V.* pp. 90–91.

indissolubility of hope, of faith, and of charity."[1] And a little later, he declares: "Anguish is not and cannot be the last word. I should be so bold as to say, on the contrary, that the last word must be with love and joy."[2] That this is no empty rhetoric or merely wishful thinking, our inquiry into the nature of the ordeal that tests fidelity and the manner of its actively surmounting it through faith and hope testifies. Equally it has shown that love is the soul of fidelity; for at each stage of the ordeal, there has been required from fidelity that stead-fast recognition and wholehearted acceptance of the person as person which is possible only in love.

Love is a word as liable to debasement as any in common currency. Like any other word it is only in its mint condition that it retains its especial value. Since love is a concept used of persons, it is in the personal context that we shall find it in that condition. And this straightway means that it is divested of any possessive significance. It also means that love in its essence is a spiritual act. It is equally true that the love of human persons must be embodied. But what we have found to be true of embodiment and what we have found to be true of presence show that while the ambiguity of a condition that is at once carnal and spiritual carries within it the perpetual possibility of its reduction to one or other aspect, this is no more necessary than it is licit. Thus, while Marcel recognizes that "many souls marked by Jansenism have yielded to the temptation of renouncing the human and deserting the earth, without for all that getting any nearer to heaven," he equally asserts that "man will never be on a par with animals: where he is himself, where he remains faithful to his calling, he rises infinitely above that level; where he deliberately renounces his mission, he falls infinitely below it."[3] Love, therefore, even in its most intimately physical expression remains a spiritual act, embodied certainly, but manifesting in that embodiment its spiritual presence which, if recognised, transfigures the physical element.[4] In order, therefore to understand even physical love as love, we must understand what it is that love itself is.

We can consider the question of what the concept of love means in the personal context under three main headings. What is the nature of the exigency that love fulfils? What is the mode of its fulfilling that exigency? And, what is the peculiar mark that signifies its fulfilment and so distinguishes love from the other themes of presence? The

---

[1] M.E. II. p. 171.
[2] M.E. II. p. 178.
[3] H.V. pp. 127–128.
[4] H.V. pp. 117–118.

answer to the first query is quite simply that love fulfils the exigency for being on the level of fully conscious presence. "Love as the breaking of the tension between the self and other appears to me to be the essential ontological datum."[1] Thus, "love rises up like an appeal from the I to the I"; "I do not love (someone) because of what he is, I love what he is, because he is himself, I thus boldly anticipate all experience; I anticipate all the predicates in which experience will be deposited"; "there is an act, a state, a manner of being, as you will, which can be likened by the descriptive consciousness to the recognition of a predicate, but in reality it is an enrichment of my being."[2] What this means is that love reaches out to the *ipseity* in personal reality – beyond any *taleity* it exhibits – that is to the person precisely as person, as participating with me in being. "The reality of the loved being is essential in love; there is no (subjective) truth that can transcend that reality. In this sense it is perhaps true to say that only love is real knowledge and that it is legitimate to associate love and adequate knowledge, in other words that only for love is the individuality of the beloved immune against disintegration and crumbling away, so to speak, into the dust of abstract elements. But it is only possible to maintain the reality of the beloved because love posits the beloved as transcending all explanation and all reduction. In this sense it is true to say that love addresses itself to what is eternal."[3] The "proof" of these assertions can evidently only be by way of recognition, since love, being personal, cannot be understood from the outside. The recognition is clarified precisely in exposing love to the ordeal that calls into question the significance and the value of the presence affirmed by love to be beyond any objective criticism or evaluation. This clarification we have already carried out in the case of belief and hope, which are now seen to be essentially modes of loving; that is, when pushed to their limits, belief and hope bear on the identical reality which is affirmed in loving. In this sense, love cannot be mistaken; it is not blind. This does not mean that love cannot be mistaken in the particular qualities it discerns in the beloved. But the lover is in a much better situation to recognise the essential value and reality of his beloved than anyone else. Similarly, any objective information about the beloved is certainly information about that person; but it is not directly relevant to the deepest significance of that person and to share in that significance it must be integrated into an awareness of the person *qua* person

[1] *B.H.* p. 167.
[2] *J.M.* p. 217.
[3] *J.M.* p. 63.

that is precisely love.[1] This suggests that love is most fully love when it is reciprocal between fully mature persons. There is, of course, a tutelary love – such as that of the parent, the educator, the physician, the psychiatrist – but this is itself dependent on love in the fuller sense and orientated towards the development of the child, patient, or pupil, in its *trust* to that point where it is capable of mature love, which only them will be fully free. On this point, Marcel has drawn attention to the interesting fact of the ontological significance of weakness in the personal context. The claim for protective love which any civilisation worth its salt recognizes in the weak, the defenceless, the enfeebled, is grounded in the ontological value of the person and the fact that recognition of this value embraces the recognition that it is an exigential value, not fully realised, upon whose active fostering depends the very value of the persons and the community of persons to whom the appeal is made in the very recognition of the weakness.[2] Of course, insofar as we never measure up fully to our ontological exigency, we all stand in some need of this protective love: we are never, as persons, fully mature in this world.

The answer to our second query is by now obvious. Love fulfils the exigency that animates it through belief, hope and fidelity. At the same time, connected with this question or, more exactly, involved in it, there is another question bearing on the way persons recognize the presence of other persons. (We deliberately do *not* say "recognize other minds" no more than we should say "recognize other bodies," these being abstract concepts objectively specifying "person.") But this question too has been in principle already answered. There was, we saw, no obstacle to the manifestation of presence in the physical element of perception. Similarly, there was no obstacle to recognizing in that manifestation a peculiarly spiritual element. Both are present together. "Spiritual perception" is not superadded to "physical perception," neither is it a parallel process. It pervades the latter and envelopes it. That is to say that love is at once perception and emotion, knowledge and affectivity."[3] It is affective knowledge and perceptive emotion. And this amounts to saying that love is the full recognition and welcoming of presence in which truth and value come home in being. It is only in talking about love in objective terms that we tend to separate and to keep separate features that in our concrete and personal experi-

[1] Needless to repeat that the presence recognised in love is the person as *ipseity*, a presence pervading any specific qualities referred to it.
[2] From a letter to the author, September 1959.
[3] *J.M.* p. 63.

ence are manifest as features of one living reality. But, if we cannot help talking about it in this way? yes, but we can help thinking of it so, as Marcel's metaproblematic mode of reflection shows.

We can, then, turn to the question of what is the distinctive feature of loving that marks it as *the* fulfilment of ontological exigency and as *the* adequate recognition of presence – in short, as creativity *par excellence*. The clue to its answering lies in two remarks made by Marcel himself: "Being is expectancy fulfilled to overflowing, the experience of being is fulfilment" and "Joy is not the mark of being but its very upsurge. Joy – fullness."[1] The relevance of joy to our understanding of the concept of personal love is clear, once we grasp its relevance to the themes of presence and fulfilment. Happiness, Marcel pertinently remarks, is a mode of self-presence and this is clarified by the further reflection that to act joyfully is to enter into one's activity with one's whole self.[2] For, joy must not be confused with satisfaction nor identified with self-enjoyment into which it contracts only in the measure of our exclusive introversion. Joy, in fact, is expansive – a being *with*.[3] This becomes clear, once we understand the connection between joy and giving that is effected through generosity. Marcel's definition of generosity is *"a light whose joy is in giving light, in being light."*[4] And for "light" one can substitute "presence" in its essential quality of creative "manifestivity" and "expansivity." Now, love is a way of being present that is joyful and generous, that delights in giving. More importantly, what is given in love is not this or that particular gift but – through, in, and with the gift – the giver himself. "Any gift is in some way a giving of oneself, and... however difficult it may be to think of a gift of oneself, such a gift cannot on any account be likened to a transfer."[5] Objects are transferred from one objective locus of ownership and control to another. While the gift *as* gift is not materially altered by its giving, *as* gift it is invested with a symbolic significance that is wholly derived from the non-symbolic gift of oneself *as* presence that is involved in loving. How this gift of presence can be creative, we have seen in considering the various themes of presence that, as such, are equally themes of that invocation of the other as a person – as *thou* and not *as him* – which is precisely love. Joy is at once the impulse, the informing spirit, and the flower of that generosity which is, as Marcel rightly

[1] *M.E.* II. p. 46; *J.M.* p. 230.
[2] *J.M.* pp. 230, 280.
[3] *M.E.* II. p. 120.
[4] *M.E.* II. pp. 119–120.
[5] *M.E.* II. p. 119.

affirms, itself the soul of giving. In this light, joy has with presence much the same relationship that we found to be had by charm. If anything distinguish them, it might be that charm seems to refer to the effect of presence on the recipient, while joy refers to its active source. A further basis for distinction might be seen in the interval lying between the experience of charm and its acceptance, while joy communicates itself immediately and in full vigour. We can, then, go further and say that all love involves joy as the emotional or affective aspect of its cognitive – affective unity. Joy is the acme of willing, as insight is that of knowing. That both be present in loving, so that presence is not complete – as communicated or communicating – until it be acknowledged joyfully, only means to say that love is the supreme awareness of which the person in the full exercise of his creative powers is capable. To love someone is to rejoice in being with them and in that joyful recognition of their personal being to be – and to be with them – more fully.

There is no need to make apology for the recognition that love is an experience privileged with respect to any other. There is no need to apologize for seeing in it the one fully adequate recognition of personal reality as such and the activity which invests the person with his peculiar dignity and in which is realised his true value. Nor need there be any hesitancy in asserting that the affective and the cognitive aspects of loving are of equal importance in assessing its true character. Experience reflected upon metaproblematically leads to no other conclusion. Any other mode of awareness or any other form of evaluation reaches the personal as such only in the measure that it is, practically speaking, imbued with love or, theoretically speaking, recognizes what love recognizes. It might be thought, for instance, that in hate we have as certain a knowledge of the person. A little reflection dispels this illusion. Hatred, in fact, is the objective attitude, as Marcel defines it, driven to the limits of its practical expression. In hating someone, I disbelieve in his participating in any true sense in being. I despair of his deriving from that participation any value. I reject any bond between him and me. I withdraw myself from him as a person utterly. Far from recognising the person as a person, hatred may be said to see in him a disperson reduced to mere object of my hatred, if that hatred be, in fact, consistent. For, we often mistake our hatred for some defect – however grave and monstrous – in his personality for the complete rejection that is hatred's in its genuine manifestation. In fact, it is impossible to hate a person *qua* person and we can only do so by regarding him effectively as an object. Even there, our hatred is in function of some positive value with which the person hated, abstraction made from his ontological reality as person, is held to be in utter conflict. Hatred, then, is licit only with respect to specific qualities or actions of that person and in virtue of a love of universal good in which, as person, the subject of those qualities or actions is embraced. To say that to act otherwise would be in that measure to unmake ourselves as persons would be no more to moralize than does the economist who diagnoses the economic consequences of a particular economic action. The person unmakes himself as person through acting ill, as he makes himself through acting well.

Finally, we have said that love is creative. There is no difficulty, as we have seen, from the metaproblematic standpoint and bearing in mind that creation – in Marcel's precise sense of the term – is not production, in affirming that loving is an activity and, as such, an intensification of presence, in no mere abstract or metaphorical sense, – a "being more." In the final analysis, love is an affirmation of the spiritual as an order of reality, given indeed with the person as embodied, but more real than either the order of the purely material or the order of the purely ideal which are asserted by way of abstraction from the personal. That is to say, while no activity of the existing human person is disembodied there is no such activity which is not at the same time in some sense spiritual. This spiritual reality is, furthermore, the central reality of the person, most strongly present in love. Once again, it is possible from a purely problematic standpoint to deny the spiritual; just as, it is possible, as the history of philosophy testifies, to deny the physical. From the metaproblematic standpoint, the concept of person is primary and it is the concept of a being whose central reality is spiritual but which is present here and now, incarnate. Flesh and spirit translate more accurately than mind and body the terms of a non-objectifiable relationship which is, as Marcel states, *sui generis*. In this light, we see that love cannot be reduced to a more disposition. Objectively conceived, a disposition is a mere function and, as such, is conceivable only with respect to a non-functional reality which, in the final analysis, is the person – spirit enfleshed. There is, of course, a dispositional use of "love." But the disposition must be understood in terms of a real disposing of the entire person to actual loving. Like any of my dispositions, it is, to use the phrase employed by Marcel with reference to memory, incorporated into my being. That is to say that is disposes my whole being, flesh and spirit, in appropriate manner, to further intensifying my presence in the world and that this presence, while carnal and spiritual at once, is most importantly spiritual.

"Something is placed in jeopardy from the moment I exist, but which can also be saved and it *will be* only on condition of its being saved... it is my soul."[1] This is the *essential* reality in the person. Treating of the question whether through invocation of the other as *thou* – that is, through love – I apprehend the essence of the person more directly, Marcel notes the extreme ambiguity of the term "essence." "By essence we can understand either a nature or a freedom." And he continues; "It is perhaps of my essence *qua* freedom to be able to conform myself *or not* to my essence *qua* nature. *It may be of my essence to be able not to be what I am;* in plain words, to be able to betray myself."[2] "Essence *qua* freedom" is in fact the soul considered precisely as free to accept or reject its "essence *qua* nature" – "what I am" – in other words my ontological exigency. As ideal to be fulfilled, essence is invoked elsewhere by Marcel thus: "Combine the idea of essence with the idea of universe. The essence regarded as the highest point of a certain universe. The idea of 'summit' could perhaps be replaced with the idea of 'the centre.'"[3] The two terms are, in fact, strictly correlative. Macrocosmically speaking, the essential is that Being in which I with my fellows participate: microcosmically, it is "my being." As "summit" of the universe I am, my essence is the ontological ideal that is personal fulfilment of my essence as "centre." This "centre" is source of the existential exigency for that ideal and heart of the presence that, in growing measure approximates it and is my actual being as a whole, my person. In the end, then, within the personal context, being, essence, and existing are integral and indissociable aspects of my person. The more I exist, the more I am, the more essentially myself, the more truly person. The distinctive feature that existing introduces is my being incarnate. But, then, as human person I can be said to bear within me an essential exigency for this incarnation; so that, while I must still be said to be when disembodied but not strictly to exist, this being is lacking something essential to its fullness, though *not* the most essential without which I would not continue to be nor ever could have been at all. Being and existing, moreover, we have seen to be essentially intersubjective: *co-esse* and *co-existens*. "The more my existence takes on the character of *including* others, the narrower the gap becomes which separates it from being; the more, in other words, I am."[4] Love is the final and most

[1] *J.M.* p. 282.
[2] *B.H.* p. 106.
[3] *B.H.* p. 57.
[4] *M.E.* II. p. 35.

effective closing of this gap. And since the person is essentially a "being more" through being more *with* other persons, love is the essential creative act. Love, we can say, is the meaning of the person. The person exists to love. Within the fellowship of being that love creates and sustains, the person *is* most fully.

CONCLUSION

Concluding our inquiry into the meaning of the concept of person in the philosophy of Gabriel Marcel, we can with justice say that this concept is the focal concept of that philosophy. It is, we have found, the concept of a being, existing in the world, incarnate but, as participating in Being in an appropriately personal manner, transcending the world of things and impersonal existents and conscious of so doing. As the concept of a being that participates personally in Being, it is the concept of a being that is at once distinct from, yet capable of being directly present to, in varying degrees of intensity, those with whom he so participates. As the concept of a being that is essentially incarnate, it is the concept of a being in immediate pre-reflective communion with the world in which he is situated and thereby predisposed to the fuller communion of personal awareness. As the concept of an incarnate person it is the concept of a spirit, enfleshed indeed, but which in and through its physical receptivity and activity is equally spiritually receptive to and active as an effective presence in the world. It is the concept of a being that is not merely productive in the world but also creative of his own increasing presence – and with that of his presence to others – and co-creative of the presence of his fellows – and with that of his own. This creative action – which in the personal context is one continual creative activity, though variable in intensity – is essentially free. Its freedom, appropriated and ratified in fidelity, is grounded in belief, sustained in hope, and fulfilled in love. Equally, as the concept of a being that is essentially free, it is the concept of a being whose essence, exigentially present from the first, in some degree continually fulfilled, can yet be missed and must be saved. Again, as the concept of an incarnate being, it is the concept of a being who through physical maldisposition can be frustated, here and now, from the full development of his personality, in the ontological sense; as through the spiritual maldisposition issuing from the misuse of his freedom he can frustrate himself from achieving that personal fulfilment which is the first meaning of the concept of freedom in the personal context. It is the concept of a being essentially in situation – and therefore not adequately intelligible without that reference – but who as situated is on the move, so that his situation is an essentially developing one. It is the concept of a being whose irreducible *ipseity* is equally an exigency for transcendence, a transcendence – at once vertical and horizontal – which is experienced as the fulfilment of that exigency. It is, moreover, a *synidesic* concept whose meaning is recognised within recollection of himself as a whole through a meta-problematic reflection which recuperates the integrity dissolved by objective thinking. By that reflection, which is personal in the strictest sense, the aspects objectivized by problematic reflection, are not merely re-synthesized but re-interpreted metaproblematically with reference to the person in his strictly unspecifiable reality – which *qua* charac-teristics, those specific aspects presuppose – and in that context viewed in their non-objective relationship with each other. It is a concept, therefore, whose essential meaning is always present but susceptible of indefinite deepening, both in itself and in its application to individual persons. Since its essential meaning holds for all persons, while it is not derived by abstract generalization, it can be said to be a concept that is concretely universal. Finally, the concept, like the reflection from which it issues and the existential experience from which both derive, is, simultaneously and indissociably, emotionally and intellectually significant – indeed, only thereby fully significant.

All this means that the concept of person is not just one of a family of concepts, but itself, so to speak, progenitor of such a family, each concept of which must be interpreted as it behaves within the family circle that is its home, note taken of its family likeness. Similarly, the meaning of those affiliated concepts, so understood in their filiation, is relevant to the meaning of the progenitor concept itself. That is why an understanding of this concept, as Marcel conceives it, is essential to an adequate understanding of his philosophy as a whole. This does not mean, of course, that the concept of person, as we have analyzed its meaning metaproblematically, is formally and specifically the subject of every reflection in Marcel's Journals or the explicit theme of each discourse he delivers or of each essay he writes. But, we submit, on the evidence of our inquiry, that it is this concept which is the starting point, and destination of his investigations as a whole, as it is its per-vasive concern, precisely because it is the total question from which problematic inquiry abstracts while presupposing it, and which is acknowledged by Marcel, as we have seen, as a prior issue to any concern with Being. This is the central concept that expresses and directs

Marcel's philosophical interests, the question that has led him to undertake the kind of investigation he has undertaken. The fact that he has not undertaken a systematic investigation starting from this concept is due to many reasons, nonetheless connected. In the first place, given the philosophical climate he grew up in and the rationalistic, positivist, and idealist philosophies against which he reacted, in protest against their misconstruing of experience, it is not surprising that he was chary, as were to be so many others on both sides of the Channel, of systems as such. Nonetheless, it was this mistrust that led him to examine critically and originally the whole basis of objective systematization in the way he has done and which has allowed, if not of recasting his thought in a system of serially derived and objectively stated propositions, then of disengaging a concept from which his inquiry in fact issues and whose central concern so manifestly harmonizes its various themes. In the second place, given this underlying harmony, it is one which, growing with the progress of his investigations, is more easily recognized at this later point of his development. Granted his own overriding urge to explore yet unchartered zones of experience, it is not surprising that Marcel has not taken time off to recollect the journey so far made in the light of its central concern.[1] All the more important, then, to have undertaken the task of recollecting his philosophic inquiry in that light and to have related therein the various themes through which he approached this focal insight. This is especially necessary, if one would approach his various and, except for the Gifford Lectures, formally disconnected treatments of distinct themes with the necessary sympathy to understand what he says and correlate their several insights. Approaching each theme afresh, with a fresh audience in mind, has led to some overlapping and reiteration of ideas on Marcel's part.

We have mentioned the Gifford Lectures. There, by nature of the occasion, the central concern is religious and the focal concept that of Being. This provides no contradiction with our claim concerning the concept of person. For, it is from this question that Marcel himself has approached the religious question and it is the question of "who am I" that he rightly sees as the starting point for any inquiry into the meaning of Being. That such is the case would seem to follow from the recognition, implicit in the affirmation of the person as such, of his participating in Being. While, however, our understanding of the concept of Being – insofar as this be thought in distinction from its manifestation as participated in – depends upon our understanding of the concept of

[1] C.f. *P.E.* p. 96.

person – which is that participation – the latter question can be pursued without pursuing the former to its ultimate conclusion. If then this question of what Being in itself might be is to have any meaning – and while we deliberately refrain from raising it as beyond our inquiry's scope, it is clear that it can issue neither in pure monism nor in sheer pluralism – it will only do so, if we approach it from within the concrete and existential situation of being a person. This conclusion is reinforced by the earlier one that impersonal existing as such can only be adequately approached within the same context.[1] Since, as we have seen, the person as person stands at the periphery of the problematic world and of the language used to express it, while being in itself is meaningful only when approached from within the personal context, it follows that problematic inquiry is not competent to settle this question, either by denial or affirmation, or by declaring it meaningless. From within the personal context, which all problematic inquiry presupposes, the question is certainly meaningful. The question of the varying merits of the attitudes that can be adopted with regard to the question of Being in itself is not, strictly, within the scope of this present inquiry and cannot, therefore, be brought into play to invalidate its affirmation of the personal, since they are possible only starting from it.

This again indicates the value of Marcel's understanding of the concept of person for philosophic inquiry as such. With regard to the affirmation of such a concept, our inquiry has led us to recognize in it an affirmation possible only within the context of our concrete existential experience, recollected as a whole and metaproblematically reflected. In that context, so recollected and so reflected, the appropriate concept of the person, whose nature we have outlined and whose essential meaning we have disengaged, is subject of *recognition* and not of objective demonstration, for the precise reasons which Marcel gives and with which we have been led to agree. Disagreement is possible and, even, apparently justifiable, if one interprets experience problematically. But it is difficult to see how such interpretation can justify itself. It comes down to a mere assertion that my experience is not such and it is on y a question that in the end can be settled for oneself. An *argumentum* ¹a *multitudine* is only an extension of a decision which is essentially opinion or conviction infused with a *hyperdoxal* element. Indeed, such disagree-

---

[1] Hence, Marcel's lack of concern with philosophic cosmology. Apart from the acknowledgement of their existing, the interest which impersonal existence provide is a function of personal interest as such and in itself best pursued by the methods of scientific inquiry. Marcel is not the philosopher to dictate to scientists about the use of purely scientific concepts within a scientific context.

ment, unless merely terminological, is possible only if one abstracts from personal experience as such and regards oneself impersonally as an object. From such a standpoint, however, the question of the person *qua* person does not even appear meaningful: it cannot, then, be raised, let alone denied or affirmed. To add that problematic reflection, the attitude informing it, and the language in which it is expressed cannot justify themselves, but only what is determined within them in virtue of controlling interests that are simply accepted, is but to reassert what most philosophers have been led to recognize. It is Marcel's peculiar contribution to the question to show how and what, in fact, this functional view of reflection and language presupposes, whether it chooses to recognize the fact or not. For, the question of the person as a person, – as participating, therefore, in Being – is the sole meaningful total question. And this is true, even if we suppress the question of what that Being is in which they participate. For inquiry, speech, and human action are carried on by persons in a personal context. Thus, to recognise persons as among the basic particulars in the conceptual scheme we actually operate is, from the metaproblematic point of view not good enough. It is always open to the objection that there might be other conceptual schemes. And from the purely problematic standpoint this objection is justified, since problematic schemes are defined in function of a controlling interest freely adopted. Moreover, to say that persons are such particulars is, at the most, to recognise that they are realities presupposed by any specification without drawing any conclusion from this fact as to the essential meaning of the concept. To assert that there could he no other meaning than that they are points of objective reference is, for reasons already given at length, an arbitrary procedure. On the other hand, from the metaproblematic point of view, not only is such a decision seen to be arbitrary but also why it is so; not only can inquiry proceed meaningfully to the question of the essential meaning of the concept, for it is only from there that can be understood what an essential meaning might signify, but the acceptance of persons as primary – in fact, *the* primary – particulars of any personal conceptual scheme – and it is hard to see how any other could have more than merely speculative value – is justified. Our games of interpreting symbols through other symbols may be interrupted by experience, but only metaproblematic inquiry – whatever the terminology it employ or the name given it – can discover what, in fact, that experience is.

Metaproblematic inquiry, leaves problematic inquiry master in its own domain. Its criticism of such inquiry only concerns and rightly concerns its attempts to deny the metaproblematic and personal order within which it is carried out or the equally unjustified assumptions about the meaning of the person *as such* which it might make without effecting the necessary change of attitude and employing the appropriate mode of reflection. For, as we have seen, the person does not enter *as such* into problematic inquiry of any kind: though it can be the *de facto* subject of any such inquiry. Nor is there from within problematic inquiry as such, any hope of adequately integrating the various characteristics defined by the specific forms such inquiry takes and which happen to bear on the person. Such an integration requires the reference of those characteristics to and their *synidesic* correlation within the concept of person *qua* person. The fact that this should be the concept of a human person does not affect the issue; since what might be or mean a non-human person could only be approached by us through an understanding of what it means to be a human person.

A final merit of Marcel's acceptance of the concept of person is that so understood the concept is restored its full moral weight. The moral is identified with the sterling human. At the same time, the human ideal is recognised to be the fulfilment in being of the individual person. Within such a philosophic context, a phenomenological analysis of moral experience can develop at once existentially adequate and universally significant. Conflicts between *is* and *ought* cease to be relevant, belonging as they do to argument that deals in objectively conceived propositions, problematically interpreted. Or rather, from the metaproblematic point of view – which in the light of our inquiry we can claim to be the genuinely moral point of view – *is* and *ought* take on a fresh and strictly correlative meaning. The *is* in question is no longer that ascribing particular descriptions or any complex of such descriptions. Neither is the *ought* in question that sponsoring the limited goals of particular actions or desires. The *is*, indeed, is the affirmation of the person *qua* person in his total actuality which, in turn, embraces the *ought* of the existential exigency that declares his radical orientation towards ontological fulfilment. And just as any particular *is* (such as that of objective description) derives metaproblematic significance and value from its relevance to the basic existential reality of the person as such, so does any particular *ought* from its relevance to the ideal which is the focus of the exigency pervading that reality. Granted, then, his acceptance of the concept of person, for Marcel all human action takes place within a moral context. The more urgent question is a practical one of deciding in a given situation whether a projected action is truly personal, that is fulfilling of the person as a person. This argument, which we must take care to free of prejudice, precedes our recognition of a given action as moral. Marcel quite clearly allows for human fallibility in the process by his recognition of the liability to err that attends any attempt at specification. Its source is the possibility of detaching the specific quality or action from the personal context within which alone it enjoys metaproblematic relevance. Only the saint, through the wisdom derived from a lived personal integrity, approaches that sureness of moral insight that allows of immediately and unerringly placing a given project within the personal and ontological order. It is, in the last analysis, a matter of following Augustine's famous injunction: *Ama et fac quod vis.*

Inquiring into the meaning of the concept of person in the context of the philosophy of Gabriel Marcel has meant inquiring into the essential significance of being a person. This significance we have found to be together moral and ontological. Understanding what it means to be a person involves understanding what a person must be in order fully to be a person. For this reason, it were mistaken to conceive Marcel's philosophy in too narrow terms of contrasting existentialism or essentialism, philosophies of freedom or philosophies of being. It cannot even, in any narrow sense, be dubbed personalist. Certain insights he shares, indeed, with other philosophers, but this is only to be expected. Such insights, however, arise within a context whose essential significance it has been his merit to have recognized. It has been his merit to have recognized not only that all thinking, all acting, all talking takes place within the personal context but to have further recognized what essentially this context is and its peculiar relevance to the way in which we must understand what takes place within it. With his concept of the person and with the significance he has found in it, at once concrete and universal, he offers a point of departure for a philosophical inquiry that can be rooted in common experience without for that being trivial, that can be profound without ceasing to be relevant to life as we must live it.

INDEX

abstraction, 20 ff, 116 ff.
"acquaintance with", 7, 48.
activity, 1, 54, 100 ff, 110, 131, 136.
affirmation, 72 ff, 121 ff.
Alexander, I. W., 52n.
alienation, 33, 101.
ambiguity, 27, 36 ff, 42 ff, 85.
appearances, 43
appreciation, 101–102
appropriation, 11, 27, 30, 33 ff, 49 ff, 86 ff, 100 ff.
art, 104.
aspects, 25 ff, 54n, 58.
assurance, existential, 90, 116, 121.
Atomism, 80.
Augustine, St., 137.
Austin, J. L., 82.
Ayer, A. J., 9n, 49n.

Basson, A. H., 49n.
beauty, 100.
behavious, 59, 101.
being, 1, 9, 11, 16, 24 ff, 33, 38, 54, 58, 62, 65, 75 ff, 90, 94, 95 ff, 128 ff, 131 ff.
Being, Philosophies of, 104, 137.
belief, 13–14, 83, 85, 112, 115, 116 ff, 121 ff.
"believing in" – "believing that", 116 ff.
Bochenski, I. M., 1n.
body VII, 24 ff, 29, 32 ff, 36 ff, 45, 49 ff, 61 ff, 86 ff, 128, 129.
Bradley, F. H., 19 ff.

Campbell, C. H., 49n.
Cartesianism, 2, 8, 9, 10.
certitude, (c.f. "assurance"), 81.
characterisation, 39 ff, 45, 46n, 60 ff, 69, 75, 78.
charm, 97 ff.
choice, 105 ff.
Christianity, 14–15.
"claiming that", 115.

commitment, 95, 101 ff, 105 ff, 114.
community, (c.f. "intersubjectivity"), 95, 125.
concepts, 28, 29, 55 ff, 131 ff.
constancy, 113.
conviction, 115 ff.
Copelston, F. C., 14n, 70n, 79n.
creativity, 33, 54, 104, 105, 110, 114 ff, 121, 122, 128 ff.

Daly, C. B., 2n.
death, 119, 121 ff.
De Finance, J., 70n.
designation, 72n.
desire, 31 ff, 106 ff.
despair, 120 ff.
Determinism, 105.
disponibility, 114 ff, 122.
disposition, 128 ff.
doxa, 115.
Drever, J., 73n.

embodiment, c.f. "body" and, 26 ff, 36 ff, 108 ff.
emotion, 34 ff, 72 ff, 81 ff, 91, 116 ff, 125.
Empiricism, 10, 12, 15.
Epiphenomenalism, 37n, 92.
essence, 100, 129 ff, 131, 137.
Essentialism, 137.
exclamatory awareness, 70 ff, 95, 96.
exigency, 53 ff, 64, 65, 75, 80, 82, 95, 102, 125, 126, 136.
existence, 5, 34, Chap III, 96, 121, 129.
Existentialism, 35n, 60, 137.

faith, c.f. "belief".
feeling, 30, 31 ff, 34 ff, 54, 72 ff, 81 ff, 91.
fellowship, c.f. "intersubjectivity" and, Chap IV.
Fichte, J. G., 10n.
fidelity, 83, 85, 112 ff, 121 ff, 131.
flesh, 128.

fulfilment, 80, 82, 94, 95, 102, 110, 131, 136ff.
functional, the, 83ff, 98, 112.

gift, 123.
Gifford Lectures, 122, 133.

Hampshire, S., 12n, 34n, 49n, 105n.
hatred, 127ff.
having, 28ff.
Hillman, J., 34, 35n, 46n, 73n, 81n, 91n, 117n.
Hocking, W., 54, 74.
hope, 83, 85, 112, 118ff, 131.
hyperdoxal, 115, 118, 134.

ideal, the, 100, 136.
Idealism, VIII, 2, 11, 19, 46, 66, 80, 133.
idée profonde, 57.
identification, 67ff, 93ff.
identity, 20, 49ff, 70, 75.
implication, 29.
incarnation, c.f. "*body*" and "*embodiment*".
indefectibility, 114, 121.
individual, 50, 69, 70, 75, 100, 109, 110, 136.
intention, 52ff, 57.
instrumentality, 33, 86ff.
intersubjectivity, 11, 46ff, 52, 54, 77, 129.
intuition, 15, 51ff.
invocation, 59, 85.
ipseity, 117.
irreducible, the, 11, 15, 37, 45, 59, 63, 64, 97, 132.
"is", 37ff, 58, 130, 136.

Jansenism, 123.
Jaspers, K., 4, 5n.
joy, 123, 126ff.
judgement, c.f. also "*affirmation*", 37ff, 98, 116.
Kant, I., 8, 9.
knowledge, 1, 125, 127.
"knowledge about", 7, 48.

language, VII, 1, 3, 42, 45, 47, 59, 65, 75, 117, 134.
Lewis, H. D., 7n.
liberté d'indifference, 107.
life, VII, 1, 101ff, 137.
literature & philosophy, 13.
love, 48, 83ff, 93, 112, 123ff, 131, 137.

MacMurray, J., 22n, 35n, 49n.
Materialism, 92.
memory, 89.
Merleau-Ponty, M., 10, 42.
metaphysics, c.f. also "the metaproblematic", 9ff, 12, 15ff, 66.
metaproblematic, the, 9ff, Chap. VI, 93ff, 105, 108, 115, 122, 132, 134ff.
Miller, B., 74n.
mind-body, VII, 36ff, 50ff, 97, 128ff.
Monism, 19, 133.
morality, VIII, 77, 99, 136.
mystery, c.f. "the metaproblematic", and, 16ff, 94.

Nominalism, 80.
Nuttin, J., 1n, 105n.

obedience, 112ff.
objectivity & objective attitude, 8ff, 24, 35, 45ff, 72ff, 96ff, 117, 132, 136.
ontological question, 38, c.f. also "*being*"
opinion, 115ff.
optimism, 119, 120.
ordeal, 111ff, 119.
"ought", 58, 136.
ownership, 32ff, 49ff.

parallelism, psycho-physical, 92.
participation, 49, 59, 61, 79, 82, 89, 95, 102, 118ff, 121, 127.
passion, 32.
past, 89, 102ff.
Paul, L., 88n.
perception, 125.
person *qua* person, knowledge of, 47ff, 93ff, 118ff, 133ff.
personal index, 22.
phenomenologial inquiry, 28, 43, 117, 136.
philosophic inquiry, 1f, 7, 19, 21ff, 42ff, 134ff.
pluralism, 20.
predication, 37ff.
predictibility, 106.
pre-reflective awareness, 12, 24, 34, 37, 45, 79ff, 89ff, 95.
presence, 59, 75, 76ff, 83ff, 92ff, 96ff, 103, 105, 113, 121ff, 125ff.
problematic, the, 9ff, 22, 26, 51, 93ff, 115, 13ff.
problematic inquiry, 93ff.
profile, 70.